THE SILENT VICTIM

TESTIMONY OF A NOBODY

LEAH LOVELACE-SQUARE

 TRILOGY

Trilogy Christian Publishers
A Wholly Owned Subsidiary of Trinity Broadcasting Network
2442 Michelle Drive
Tustin, CA 92780
Copyright © 2020 by Leah Lovelace-Square
All Scripture quotations, unless otherwise noted, taken from THE
HOLY BIBLE, KING JAMES VERSION®, KJV® Copyright ©
1973, 1978, 1984, 2011 by Biblica, Inc.® Used by permission. All
rights reserved worldwide.

For information, address Trilogy Christian Publishing
Rights Department, 2442 Michelle Drive, Tustin, Ca 92780.
Trilogy Christian Publishing/ TBN and colophon are trademarks of
Trinity Broadcasting Network.
For information about special discounts for bulk purchases, please
contact Trilogy Christian Publishing.
Manufactured in the United States of America

Trilogy Disclaimer: The views and content expressed in this book
are those of the author and may not necessarily reflect the views
and doctrine of Trilogy Christian Publishing or the Trinity Broadcasting Network.

10 9 8 7 6 5 4 3 2 1
Library of Congress Cataloging-in-Publication Data is available.

ISBN 978-1-64088-935-4
ISBN 978-1-64088-936-1 (eBook)

I would like to honor a lady that was like an angel in my life. You brought out the best in me. You were an essential part of the foundation in my life, and without that foundation, I would have remained lost. You weren't perfect and never claimed to be; however, your character demonstrated an essence of perfection that goes untouched. Your humility, meekness, patience, lessons, love for your family, passion to teach, and firmness in what you believed in helped me to know who I was even when I felt lost. You were in my thoughts when I fought so hard to come out of my mess. You were there when I struggled the most and helped me to pick up the pieces when I fell. You were there through my sickness. You were there in my darkest hour praying over my life. Thank God, you were there to witness the goodness of the Lord working in my life and through my deliverance. You will always be in my heart, and the lessons you taught will remain a part of me. Thank God for you, my grandmother, my Nanny, Ruby Mae Williams. I will always love you. Thank you!

Rest In Peace

Table of Contents

CHAPTER 1

The Plan

A few years back my cousin and I were sitting on the sofa in her living room. Just two ladies sharing some time together while the kids played in the back room, not talking about much, when she asked me so openly, "What made you go this way after all these years?" She was referring to the decision I had made to follow the way of Jesus Christ. It stunned me. That moment I realized that it wasn't just a decision I had made but an action that others had come to notice. I had never given thought to it in the past because my decisions and actions I had made in Christ had been an instinct and not a thought-out plan. However, very easily, almost with the same response I had when I got up and gave my life to Christ, I answered my cousin, "Because I gave enough of my life to the ways of Satan." Right then, at that very moment, the spirit of God released revelation in me. I had given myself to the devil! I did! Not my parents or the situations I had gone through. The struggles and heartache I had experienced wouldn't have given me a first-class ticket to hell. The decision I made in my past was determining my future, and by the grace of God, there was a way out. Thank God, I found the way out!

"What happened," I thought, "that pushed me into that path to hell to begin with?" I had always been a spiritual person, I thought. I wasn't in church praying, or fasting on a regular basis; however, I had a strong belief in God. I knew who He was. I had faith that He was the only way to heaven. I had situations that happened to me like everyone else, but it shouldn't have given me enough ammo to fall from grace. I thought I was on the right track. I was not saved yet; however, I made plans to be when I got myself together. When I was complete with living my young adult life and having a few more experiences, I would have been ready to give my life to Christ.

I had enough understanding to what that meant. My parents, grandparents, aunts, and uncles had shown me the way of living for the Lord. I was exposed to the Bible before I could read fluently. I was in church periodically and knew what to do and whom to go to when I needed understanding of the Bible. I knew how to pray and prayed very often. I even had enough wisdom to know to pray when seeking anything because the Lord was who supplied my needs. However, when I looked back on my life, all that I knew was so distant from me during that dark time. It was as if a wall had been built between me and the truth, and the conscience that I once had that convicted me in the past was no longer there to make me hesitate when I was going too far. I stepped too far away from what I knew and stepped into unfamiliar territory without any protection, any good judgement, and not enough faith to be pulled back from experiences that I should never had been tainted with. I was lured into a mindset that literally opened the gates of Hell in my life, and I was at a point of no return! I became a victim to the work of the enemy, and the shame

I had within myself was greater than my belief in life after the decisions I had made.

Shay was his name! He was the last good thing in my life that I could remember. We met my senior year of high school in Baumholder, Germany. It was about late winter when I was working at a fast food restaurant that I noticed this soldier coming to my counter every evening ordering the same shrimp and fries basket from Popeye's. Though he hung out with a wilder group, Shay had a calmness about him that I found so interesting. He didn't have the demeanor of the typical young men enlisting into the military that I had gotten accustom to being around and honestly couldn't stand. Being raised in the military as an Army brat since I was four years old, I felt very educated on understanding the different maturity levels of the soldier. Having a boss for a daddy, "Bulldog Lovelace" is what they called him, most men kept their distance anyway. From my experience, I didn't find soldiers very attractive. I was aware that I really was not in their lane nor up to their speed. I wasn't infatuated in the lifestyle of being a military wife as many spoke about as I grew up. Even my mother found it exciting to possibly be the mother-in-law of a military son. I was a senior. I had some plans, and though I felt I was growing distant from my boyfriend, we were still an item at the moment. Still I found myself day by day noticing this Shay. After some time passed and almost immediately after I found myself living the single life from the break up, Shay became more than just a soldier passing by my restaurant daily. He became my first real soldier friend, and we quickly grew into a couple.

I was surprised by the way Shay handled our relationship. He wasn't quick to rush anything physical between us. Our phone time was very fair, though he had a full career, and I hadn't even begun my adult life yet. He was so respectful of my family. He would always mention how he must stay on Mom's good side and make sure not to disrespect Dad. Shay changed my thought process of what I thought to be the typical soldier, always hunting for the next girl to take advantage of and throw away. Never looking for anything serious, and if marriage did come to be, adultery was a sure thing to follow. Less often did I share my thoughts with others on my judgment of the typical soldier; however, it was there and strong. Shay really changed that in me and even made me feel bad having such thoughts about others before getting to know them. Our relationship was surprisingly good, and as we grew closer to graduation, I started to think what would happen to us. Shay had a career, a tour commitment in Germany, and wasn't close to end of his tour. I was on my way to hair school in West Pennsylvania for two years. It would have been much more feasible to find that we would only be a few hours away if Shay was back in his hometown of Baltimore, but this was Germany and the military. How likely were we to keep our relationship strong stretched across an entire sea? Yet, there was still plenty of time to think about that. I still had a few more months before graduation, and who knew what would happen as June grew closer?

It was getting close to Baumholder Days, which was a military celebration on post. To me it was just another opportunity for people to come together and party. Fun, but to me it was bittersweet. Of all my closest friends, I only had two left on post with me. The memory of the year before was so emotional for me. Six of us grew into a sisterhood that started winter of 1995. We didn't know at the time that we would have grown so close, but once we all found each other, nothing separated us. With the other three back in the states, it felt so odd and with Baumholder Days drawing near. It made me think about graduation. I had been waiting my whole life for graduation; however, it meant that I was leaving shortly after. My plans were to leave at the end of June. When I made the plans earlier in the school year, I never thought I was going to meet this amazing man and actually fall for him. I had other plans, but I thought God had a better one. I tried not to think about it, but I couldn't help it. Still, Shay and I spoke about Baumholder Days like two kids getting ready for the county fair in Bristol, Pa to return.

It was finally here: Baumholder Days! I can't remember how long the festival went on, but I do remember that Shay and I were there every night I didn't work. We didn't do much but walk and talk, really about nothing, like usual; however, conversation changed those nights. He and I began talking about our future and what it would be like. It was only a few weeks before that I found out about Shay's daughter. She was back in Baltimore, and he longed to be able to get full custody over her. Shay never mentioned anything bad about her mother but made it clear that his intention was to raise her on his own. Shay's parents were caring for her while he was on his military tour.

I had always been a strong believer of having my own children. I wasn't interested in taking care of someone else's bad child. I wasn't interested in being responsible for someone else's offspring! As bad as it sounds, I was sure that I was going to have my two boys and two girls, with the oldest being a boy, by my husband's and my own doing. However, when Shay told me that he had a daughter and asked me if it would be a problem, my heart warmed with love from a picture of a girl I didn't even know. Another immediate change of heart in my life, and I wasn't afraid to tell Shay. While walking around at Baumholder Days, I got to know even more about Shay. He was so headstrong about his plans to be in the military and take care of his daughter. He was very much in love with his mom and honored her greatly. He went through a lot as a young adult but felt that the military was his opportunity to clean up, and he worked very hard to make a name for himself. I explained to Shay my love for loyalty. I had faith in the future, to be a wife, a mother, and most importantly to walk with my husband and not behind him or in front of him. I wanted Shay to know that though I was very stubborn but driven, I fight hard for anything I believe in, and at that time I believed in us.

There were three days remaining for Baumholder Days when Shay and I walked by this game. The concept was to purchase these tickets that had random numbers with a goal to collect a total of 100 points. The prize for 100 points was any giant toy at the top. I wasn't much of a gambler in any aspect, so though my eyes were stuck on this large, green mouse, I couldn't help but to weigh out the odds of costs of these tickets and the chances of winning. Slim to none; however, Shay seemed to take interest with my interest in the stuffed animal. He purchased a few tickets, and we opened them, hoping to have a good number of points; however, no luck, and after a little while and some money, I asked Shay to stop. We walked around the park a little longer and came back to the game once again. So, Shay, taking another chance, purchased some more tickets; however, no success to getting to that 100 points. We called it a night and went back to his barrack. There we spoke more about our future. We discussed how close Philadelphia was to Baltimore and how easy it would be when he came to visit for us to hang out. We spoke about when he came back from his tour, where we would end up. He was interested in doing a tour to Hawaii, and I made it very clear that I would love to be on that tour with him. I told him that I really cared about him, and though I was young and hadn't graduated high school yet, I knew what love was and loved him. I was surprised to hear that Shay loved me back. I wasn't expecting to hear that. Still, I'm sure my face lit up like a firecracker in smiles from ear to ear as he grabbed my chin and drew near to kiss me so gently. On the way home, it was so quiet. I was almost nervous; however, it was one of the most beautiful nights that I ever experienced.

The next day, to my surprise, when I walked in the door to my house late in the afternoon, I found Shay at my dining room table with my dad and my brother, searching through what looked to be hundreds of little pieces of paper. Shay had gone back out to the carnival to the game and spent more money on those tickets. It was so funny to watch as they opened the tickets looking for a combination to lead to 100 points. The focus was unreal, and the determination was so impressive. Unfortunately, the tickets never added up to the points needed to get the stuffed mouse. The missing number needed was a ticket with a number one, which I am sure was the reason no one ever won.

That night, Shay and I went out to the last night just to enjoy one another. We didn't know what to expect the following year. I might not even have the opportunity to return during that time, so we wanted to take advantage of the time we had. We must have gone by the game ten times when finally, Shay couldn't take it. Against my blessing, Shay went to buy another group of tickets. Though I was so annoyed that he was being careless with his money, I felt special that it meant so much to him. So, we opened the tickets together to find nothing! I'm not sure it if was pity or the fact that the man running the game admired Shay's determination to get me that stuffed animal, but before knew it, Shay was asking me what color and what animal I wanted. I was so excited to pick out my Army green mouse. Shay just didn't understand. "Green, Leah? You picked a green mouse?!" I told him that it was my favorite color and reminded me of him, which seemed to be negotiable terms for me to keep the green mouse.

I began counting days like my life depended on it. Prom was approaching, which meant that graduation was also approaching. Shay and I didn't make plans to go to prom. I had made plans to with my ex, and though we were no longer a couple, we had made plans almost a year prior. With my dress being made from scratch from an inspired look I saw Toni Braxton wear on an award show and my ex's Chinese tailored suit, there were no exceptions to whose arm I was going to be holding that night. Shay had no jealous bone in his body, or he was extremely cocky and not capable to show his true thoughts. He had no care in the world that I was going with my ex and actually encouraged for us to go together. I was happy to hear that because we might have had an argument about it. I waited twelve years of school to go to prom and invested a lot of thought and planning towards it.

I was one of those girls always dreaming about specific events growing up, and prom was one. Though I did everyone's hair for previous proms, I was asked each year and watched my friends as they attended prom in 10th and 11th grade, I thought it special to go to prom only once. The year I was to graduate would be the first and last prom of my life. To be thought out carefully, planned accordingly, and special. Well my plans did not go preciously the way I imagined it, since I would be walking into prom on the hand of my ex while my boyfriend waited for after prom to pick me up, but I guess nothing is perfect. Still, Shay did promise to pick me up afterwards and take me to the after party.

It was nice! It took so long for me to get myself together. Not because I take forever to get ready for much, but I was all booked up with hair appointments. I was overwhelmed to realize what I had gotten myself into. I started early in the morning prom day and did not finish with my last hair appointment until about two hours before prom began. I had just enough time to take a shower, try to finish styling my own hair and getting dressed to be fashionable late. Much to my surprise, my mother was completely freaking out as it got closer to the time of me leaving. She could not understand why I would take the entire day getting everyone else ready and not consider myself on a day that I waited so long for. She kept making the funniest looks. Not one at all to keep her mouth shut, she had little smart comments with my last two appointments.

As I finished with my last client, in my made-up shop in my bedroom, Mom sent Dad out to get me some baby breaths to place in my hair. It was the single most special moment I had with my mother in a while. We did not have the bond that an over-dreamer girl would hope to have with her mother; however, I still was a sucker to hope for the day that we would be inseparably close. The baby breaths were perfect with my pony tail updo style, which went perfectly with the store-bought dress that I purchased a week prior to prom due to the tragic mistake that the tailor made to my originally designed dress. Nothing was right, but for me it was perfect. I had the opportunity to go to prom with my ex who had grown into a dear friend and after a few hours of spending special times with peers I had grown to love over four years in Baumholder, Germany, I stepped out of the NCO club just a little early to meet up with the love of my life as he waited for me just outside the front door.

The bungalows that all the seniors were meeting up at were about a half hour away, so Shay and I had time as we waited for prom to end and then everyone to get to the after party, so we went back to his place for a little while. I hadn't seen him all day, as Shay kept his distance all day long since I was so busy. I was weary from my day that began at five that morning; however, my adrenaline was running just because I was close to him. There was an amazing feeling that came over me each time I was around Shay. We talked about graduation approaching and the plans we had. Shay still had to complete his tour and I had a school to go to.

I decided that night that I would tell Shay that my plans had changed. I decided to ask my parents if I could stay in Germany with them for a while, get a job, and stay close to Shay. We were already discussing spending our lives together, and though I did not have a proposal or a ring, Shay had made it clear that he already had plans and knew what ring he would get when the time was right.

I didn't want to wait. I didn't want to go so far away and lose time that could be well spent getting prepared for a future in the life of the military. It made no sense to me to leave for so long to get a PA license in cosmetology when I was going to end up with him. Shay already made up in his mind to stay in the military, so I would be a traveling wife and with a readymade family. Shay's daughter was back in Baltimore but once the custody went through, his intentions were to be with his daughter. I was going to be a mom and I couldn't think only about myself any longer. I was recognizing that I was making plans with a man that had a career and a family, and I had to start thinking that way if I were to be a part of Shay's life. After some detailed conversation, Shay stopped me. He explained that I wasn't going to stop my plans for him. "If we are meant to be together, we will be together no matter what," Shay confirmed. He wouldn't allow me to even speak of the idea of changing my plans. Shay assured me that it would work out, that he would trust me, and that he would give me no reason not to trust him. I explained to Shay that as long as he stayed in Baumholder with daddy, I wasn't worried about trusting him at all. If my heart got broken, the Bulldog was coming for him regardless. After some laughter from that comment about Daddy, we left the barrack to go to the after-party hand and hand.

The after party wasn't really my cup of tea, but to celebrate the upcoming graduation with my fellow classmates, it was worth the drive. We walked around the Baumholder bungalow and said high to all my friends and classmates. I saw my ex, who looked as if he was enjoying himself. As I walked around, I couldn't help but to think back on the four-and-a-half years I spent in Baumholder,

Germany. I think the entire day had turned into an emotional rollercoaster, and I was just riding.

Entering Baumholder High the winter of my ninth-grade year as a young naive girl who only thought of herself and going through all the typical teenage traumatic issues one girl is destined to endure was an experience. I realized the faces that I saw were not going to be a few steps or miles away from my home. The reunions were not going to be every year at a nearby location of the school. We weren't being raised in a community that would sustain the essences that we created; however, due to the military life, the essence would always change every two to four years, and we were all going out there to create our own lives really without a solid foundation to return to. Baumholder would be a forever memory to us all, and though some might return just to visit, there would least likely to be one soul that would remain for us to walk back into the classroom and just hug. An adult that impacted our lives might be a phone call away; however, maybe not tangible to touch. We were all moving on and only had a few weeks remaining to be together. So though not really my type of party, I cherished that very moment.

After the seniors' fear that the parents wouldn't return for our graduation, we were all so excited that the soldiers had returned in enough time to be present for our walk across that stage. The days approaching graduation seemed to come and go so fast that I couldn't remember one day from another. All I could think about was that I was moving into the next stage of my life. My Nanny, Aunt Dino, and Aunt Willame had come all the way from America for my graduation. It was so exciting to see others in the family knowing they were going to be there. I also knew that they were coming to have the German experience; however, I put in my head that it was all for me! They went on their tours, and I continued to go to my last days of school, work, and attend my last chorus performance with Mr. Lundy leading the way.

I was so touched to receive encouragement from Mrs. Higgins, who was my cosmetology teacher for the last three years of high school. I had learned so much from her, and she helped me choose the school I was going to next. She had encouraged me to not only go for my license but to get my teacher's and instructor's license because it would open up so many opportunities as well as put my mind on a different thought pattern as I developed into adulthood. I took her advice and made plans to push through the hours required in PA to fully complete the program.

Mrs. Merrent had been my keyboard teacher and the first teacher that truly inspired me to make decisions not just based on my personal wants but the needs to get to that next level. I was so angry in Keyboarding I when she made me take off my fingernails. They were personally hand-crafted, long, beautiful, and well designed and though I was no professional in tenth grade, you couldn't tell me that from my hair styles and nails. Still, Mrs. Merrent didn't play. She was one of those teachers with a passive approach but with a bold enough statement to know that she meant business and could convince a student to do just about anything. I was mad and even cursed her out under my breath, but those nails came off. I got through Keyboarding with a B and determined not to go back into that class again, but found myself in Keyboarding II, again with Mrs. Merrant, and dared not step foot in that classroom on the first day with nails.

Mrs. Lips was one of my counselors. She was there to listen when I was having moments that I was not able to share with my closest friends. She never minds listening and gave some very good advice throughout my years there. These teachers were not the only, but some of the most impactful people in my life and like my classmates, I was leaving them for good.

I walked up and down the hallways of Baumholder high acting as if I was so excited about leaving the school, the town, and the country, but honestly, I wanted just one more year. I wasn't ready to say goodbye. I wasn't ready to leave my cheerleading team, my youth program that had escalated into the grand opening of the first teen café in Baumholder, the leadership conferences, all area parties, the GS jobs, the travel to foreign countries, and my friends. I took a lot of time that last week crying to myself. I was leaving my brother and sister for the first time in my life, and they were not even going to be easy to contact. I couldn't be there anymore to help them grow, yell at them when they messed up, embrace them when they needed a hug, or argue with them when our debatable instincts kicked in. I wasn't going to really be that big sister any longer. Every time I went into my home, it was like a fake smile would grow on my face as I saw my nine-year-old sister going about her way, my fourteen-year-old brother doing his teenage thing. The tears were good for me to recognize that my life, up to that point, had not been in vain. Though I was moving on, I had memories that I know I could keep in my heart forever. I got through challenges, and I made it out. I was completing the first big event of my life, and because I failed ninth grade the first time, it was thirteen years in the making, but I did it!

The day had finally come, and I was ready. I didn't take any hair appointments because I wanted to focus on myself that day. I wanted to enjoy Leah for the day. I wanted no limits to how the day was going to go. I really didn't have any plans but to get up, make sure my hair was done, I was dressed, and that my sister and brother were ready to go. I wasn't even worried much about Shay. He said he was going to be there, and he kept to his word. I woke up in tears for absolutely no real reason, but I had been a baby all week. The tears stopped when I realized I would have puffy eyes before I would walk down the aisle. I chose a very simple short cream dress without any sleeves. The overlay was covered in light floral with blues and pinks. When I saw the dress, I knew immediately that it was going to be the one I would receive my diploma in. I was turning into a young woman that day with plans. I was receiving my diploma, I had received words of wisdom from every teacher and adult that meant anything to me, I had my aunts there and my Nanny who never missed a beat in my life. The four most important people that I lived with my entire life were there, and I was ready. The day felt perfect.

My classmates and I sung "Wind beneath My Wings", and though horribly presented from all the tears and pauses to catch a breath from the crying and continued gasping, it was sentimental as it should have been. The 33 of us took our turns as we walked on the platform to receive the certificate that ordained us to go out into the world and own it. We were all ready! As I sat there waiting for my name to be called, I got nervous because I hadn't seen my family when I walked in. I kept searching for them, and just before it was my turn, I found them in on the high end of the auditorium. Tears formed just to see them all there just for me. At that very moment I knew I was blessed. I stood up, closed my eyes just for a moment before I took my first step up the stairs, and took a deep breath and embraced all that I knew was going to happen going forward and even what I wasn't sure about. I took my diploma and exhaled with joy.

I had no idea that the seniors had plans for a parade; however, that was the plan and having a boyfriend with a car was icing on the cake. So, we drove in the parade though the post, up the hill with Champion Village on the left of us, through Wetzel Apartments, and then I saw my brother. His silly self ran up the hill to look for our car and jumped through the window to be a part of the celebration. One of his many silly acts, but it worked. Once the parade was over, we all went back to the house to have dinner and cake. It was such a good time. Shay got a chance to get to know the aunts and Nanny a little more and then Shay and I left to spend some time together.

The next few weeks were the same. The family had left, I was finishing my last few days at work, spending time with the friends that were still in Baumholder with me, and preparing to leave. Shay and I saw each other every day. Thank God he didn't have field work during that time. The last day in Baumholder felt a little like graduation day. I was overly emotional but trying to hide my tears as much as possible. I was finally sure about Shay and me. He made plans to come and see me in the next couple of months, so it was comforting to know that soon we would see each other again.

The plane was the normal nine boring hours, but I

couldn't wait to see everyone. I couldn't wait to learn how to drive, I couldn't wait to simply be a part of my family again. It had been so long since I had seen any of my cousins, aunts, and uncles. I wasn't due to arrive at school for another few weeks, so I had time to catch up as much as possible. Shay and I spoke every few days, and I thought I would miss him more than I actually did. It felt good to spend time with the family, but I had to get focused on school. I didn't realize that the trip would take four hours. Without a car, I had no outlet, but I wasn't expected to get a car until later in the year. Nanny comforted me by telling me that she had children before she had a driver's license. I was not about to be like Nanny in that scenario, so I gave myself until twenty to get a license. In Germany, teenagers weren't able to get license until much older than Americans, and after trying to take that test once, I said I would wait until I was Americanized again. I had all I needed in Germany within just a few steps from my front door. Everyone walked almost everywhere, so it was the norm. Bristol, PA, however, was a completely different story. If you didn't have a car, you were basically stuck. I was thankful to have some family my age that drove, so I had the opportunity to get around.

The day had come to leave for school. My Nanny's friend Mr. Irvine had agreed to drive us, and we left extremely early. I couldn't for the life of me figure out why we had to leave so early. I felt like Nanny was sick of me already and just needed to release; however, I discovered that I was not at all prepared for the move-in day. When we got to Dubois, we first took a look at my small, single room to see what was provided and what was needed. I had a bed and dressers, no windows, and a kitchen and bathroom to share. We met the teachers and head teacher of the school with whom I was communicating for almost a year as I prepared from Germany.

Afterward, Nanny and Mr. Irvine took me to the closest store to purchase the fridge, mattress protector, cleaning products, school supplies, and food. It turned out to be a day, and by the time I was fully moved in, we only had time to eat dinner and say our goodbyes. That might have been the one and only time that Nanny left me that I did not cry. I knew I was in a new place, but I was ready, and she was closer to me than she had ever been when I was an army brat, so I was grateful. I had been trying to be close to my Nanny my whole life, and I was finally experiencing that. She was just a call away, and the very next day I was starting my first class in cosmetology. Nanny and Mr. Irvin drove off, and I ran upstairs to begin my adult life.

CHAPTER 2

The Fall

It was hard enough living far from my parents, also stationed in Baumholder with Shay, Nanny was in Philadelphia with most of my family, and I had chosen this secluded, remote area in Dubois, PA to go to hair school. It was after a few weeks of hair school that I thought to myself, "I couldn't be one of the normal ones who found a local school to commute from home every day." No, I had to be the one who found the single hair school in Pennsylvania that provided dorms to students and a real experience of college life while learning the trade of cosmetology. Great experience for me, though very lonely. I was used to it, being raised so far from family anyway. It was only a few weeks into the program, but I felt good knowing that I made some good friends already, and the school was fun. I had my long distant pre-paid cards to call the parents, Nanny, and Shay, and that was enough for me. There were sometimes I felt a little alone, but I was strong and felt trained having over fourteen years of experience already being daddy's child. I realized I hadn't spoken to Shay in a while. The last time I talked with him, he was getting ready to go into the field and said that he would call me when he returned. I was trying to get used to the idea that I just might end up being that military wife that I thought I would never become. I figured I should wrap my mind around it so that I wouldn't have to collect all my thoughts at once if the question was to arise of us getting married. I wanted to be prepared to give the best response and not just a simple yes!

The friends I had made were mostly local and very surprised to even see this worldly black girl living and going to school in their town. The closest that most of them got to being around my culture was this one black family that I heard so much about from everyone. I am guessing it's because they were black. It was a family of four with two sons. I had never actually seen them; however, I felt like I knew them just from the conversations from one of my classmates who went to school with the older brother. There were two other ladies that also shared my color. One was from a local town where the only Walmart was in the area, Clarion. The other one lady was from St. Lucia. She stayed in the dorms with us. Color was never a big topic for me. I was raised around so many different people and cultures growing up that I had not been exposed to the prejudice that was so well known around me. I also was such an oblivious person to such things, that more than likely I wouldn't have associated prejudiced responses with me, even if directed to me. It also wasn't a big deal to be the minority, and I assumed that many that I went to school with also did not find it odd. We all became very close and adopted one another as sisters. We had the opportunity to learn from one another, grow together, and be there for one another. It felt like another military move but this time without the parents and siblings. They all had their boyfriends and they knew of Shay, though they all could not imagine having to be without their boyfriends for so long. It was hard, and I didn't hide that.

I finally had the opportunity to speak with Shay and was so happy to hear from him. Every time I heard his voice, I would light up. He told me that he received my letter and asked if I got his yet, which I did not. I asked him what it said, and of course he wasn't going to tell me that. We talked really about nothing because I felt as if Shay was trying to hold back something. He told me that he had something for me, but it had to wait until we saw each other. To be one who loves and hates surprises all at the same time, I asked what it was. I pleaded with him to tell me, and I also told him I was convinced it was a ring, but he just kept telling me that I would see. Finally, I left it alone and just enjoyed the time we had together on the phone. He said that he went to check on Mom and Dad every so often for me, which I made him promise to do, as well as checking on my brother and sister. I just wanted to make sure they were okay. We exchanged our love for one another as we approached to our last minute on our time card. He said that he was going to the field and would call me as soon as he got back. Hanging up the phone was hard, but I looked forward to whatever was coming.

When the letter arrived, I was just getting off school, and my roommate was the one who gave it to me. There was no small box with it, so I guess I had longer to wait for my ring. We had only been together for about nine months, but it felt like a lifetime. I felt as if I deserved the ring, but I knew Shay better. He was traditional. He would have had to ask both my mom and dad for my hand, and I would have had to meet his parents in person first, as well as that baby girl. He would have wanted to get down on one knee in my presence and asked me to marry him, hoping I would shed tears so he could make fun of me after I say yes. The letter was just a simple one saying how much he missed me. He mentioned that he wanted to come and see me in a few weeks and asked me if I would have some time off during Labor Day weekend. He asked that I got back with him as soon as I could so he could make plans, so I thought in my mind to call him the next day and tell him yes. All I could think of for the rest of the day was if he was coming to propose.

That night I had the craziest dream that I was sitting in a passenger seat with a driver that had a black face. There were others in the back seat that also had black faces. As we were driving the driver lost control of the wheel, and we were in an accident. I woke up from the dream in the middle of the night thinking of how crazy that was that I couldn't see anyone's face. I was a little nervous about it because my dreams were sometimes warnings but normally much more specific with details that helped me to understand. After a few days of no news about anyone hurt or any accidents, my heart was at ease.

A few weeks had passed since Shay's letter, and we were still playing phone tag. After I called and left a message, he seemed to do the same. For about a month longer, we had not heard each other's voice, and I couldn't confirm that he could come for Labor Day. After a few attempts calling on my end, I felt that Shay had stopped making attempts on his end to call. I had to find out what the concern was, so I asked the solder who always answered the phone where Shay was. I found out he was in the field, so I knew that it wasn't on purpose that he didn't make any attempt to connect with me. When the holiday came around, I was so upset that I could have been spending it with Shay, however that was another opportunity to have full understanding to what it would be like as a military wife. I took it in stride. I also had a competition coming up at school in a week that I had to prepare for.

It was a great day that day. I was filled with confidence and pride as I took home my first blue ribbon from my hair competition in school. I was looking forward to reaching out to Nanny and my parents to tell them the good news, but honestly my heart was hoping to hear from Shay. We were still playing phone tag, and I really missed him so much. He left messages with my roommates, and I left messages with the soldiers on CQ at the barracks, so I was at peace to know he was thinking of me as I was thinking of him; however, hearing his voice was what my heart longed for. I was in my room when my roommate told me I had a phone call. I was so excited to hear Shay's voice and just knew it was him, so I popped up from my bed and dashed to my door to open it, just to cross a little threshold to the phone and to realize it was my parents on the other end. I was almost just as happy, though I had just heard from them. They asked how I was doing, but there was something different about their voices. They were so sincere and quiet. I didn't hear my brother and sister in the background, and the atmosphere got so still. I became worried and asked what was wrong. My heart dropped, and I became anxious thinking the worst about the family and my siblings, but I never would have imagined that they would be on the other end telling me that Shay was in a car accident. Shay was driving home one earlier morning and lost control of the wheel. He was in the hospital in critical condition, and his friends who were with him had minor cuts and bruises but were okay. Whispers was what I heard after that moment. Mom and Dad were talking, and I was responding and saying I was okay, but I was not. Whispers was what I heard as they tried to explain to me everything. "If I just tuned them out and only heard their voices as whispers, it would be as a dream, and I would wake up from it," I thought. I heard them say they were going to get off the phone, and I don't remember what I said, but I hung up the phone. My roommate was standing distant from me as I hung the phone up. She startled me as she asked if I was okay. I told her the situation, said I was okay and went to my room. All I felt was numbness as tears continued to go down my face. I didn't understand what happened. I heard it but I could not believe it. I was lost, alone, sick, confused, and mad. I pleaded with God. I asked that He spare Shay's life. I quietly asked that He allow everything to be okay, but doubt consumed my talk with God. I could only think the worst. I couldn't do anything but cry.

It was the middle of the night when I woke up, in shock because the feeling was still there. The whispers of my parents had grown into a loud sound as I heard them say repeatedly in my head that Shay was in the hospital. It wasn't a dream! He was really hurt. He was really in critical condition. He was really on life support. He might really die! So many thoughts ran in my head about the situation. I kept trying to reason with why something like this would happen to Shay. He was a great man, thought of as a great soldier, his friends loved him, and he worked so hard for his daughter who was in Baltimore with his parents. He was the only child and only had a daughter so there is no way that he couldn't get pass this. He didn't deserve to be in that situation. Still it was all true. Shay had broken his neck, and there was no hope that he would gain his ability to even breathe on his own again, and if so, he had a very high chance of being unresponsive.

My parents kept me updated for those few days as they waited for his mother's arrival. Mother Robinson had to make a decision that I wouldn't wish on any mother. Should she allow the machine to keep her child alive or take him off and allow his fate to be as it was going to be? Shay's mother made the decision to take him off the breathing machine. I couldn't imagine what it would be like to leave your home in America just to go to Germany not to visit and tour the country but to possibly say good-bye to your only son is unimaginable! I wasn't convinced that she could even do it until Dad called to tell me that the breathing machine was removed, and Shay didn't survive. To me those three days were death each day. I was too far for this to be happening. I couldn't hold his hand to tell him I loved him. I couldn't beg him to stay with me. I could not kiss him on his lips or stay with him in the hospital all night long. I couldn't whisper in his ear that I needed him to stay with me, and I would take care of him. I couldn't plead with him that life was worth fighting for. I couldn't do anything other than sit in this secluded town that I took myself to. I could only sit in this empty room and drown in pity as my eyes puffed up so much from all the crying until my tears dried up. All I could do was dwell in misery. At that very moment, I became lost and empty with no real reason to go on with my own life. My parents attended the funeral, and they had the opportunity to meet with Shay's mother, an experience I have not had and now would never! "The funeral was nice," my mother said. Though I tried to appreciate my parents for keeping me informed, I didn't realize that I was literally shutting down. I didn't care about the funeral or anything else. I no longer cared about anything.

I continued to go to school and be as positive as I could. I was strong to those around me because I was taught that I had an impact on others as well as a responsibility to represent myself in an ideal mannerism. So, on the outside and around everyone I was okay. I didn't freak out on the phone when speaking to family and friends, and I always tried to show as if I understood the situation and the plan God had for Shay and us all. On the outside it all looked normal, but the more I spoke about understanding, the more I verbally agreed with God's plan to take Shay home to glory, and the more I smiled, my heart grew concrete! A numbness was filling within me, and I had no outlet and no one to release to. I cried alone, I yelled alone, I was depressed, and I was in this situation alone. I was growing a hate for Shay being taken away from me. I was so angry towards God's decision for Shay's life and for Shay leaving me behind. I didn't have the opportunity to hear Shay's voice before he left. Shay just went on to be with the Lord. No fight to stay with his daughter, no fight to remain a child to his parents, no fight to be with me! And God just took Shay from me without warning. The dream was there, but not like the other dreams. Not clear enough for me to act. Not so much as an opportunity to see him again, tell Shay that I loved him, beg Shay not to leave me, demand that Shay fight. My heart for Shay and God was growing harder and harder with every attempt to speak it all better. The love was growing weary with every move I made to show myself strong. The hope was dwindling to nothingness as I sought after the Lord for answers but received nothing. My faith was fading as I came to understand that what should have been—the love, marriage, happily ever after—was never going to happen!

I had made it to a month and still surviving, but barely. Still stuck in my silence, I found my heart continuing to grow cold. I hated the fact that I was stuck lonely, always having to face life alone. Always feeling as if I had no one to really turn to concerning myself and my problems. During those lonely times in my past, I found myself closing my eyes and talking to the Lord, but I lost trust in that as well. With every dream I was having, I ignored Him. Every time I got a thought to pray, I refused the Holy Spirit's push. Every part of me that enforced the relationship with the Lord that I needed and longed for was clouded by the doubt of any true outcome. I no longer believed that my prayers were making it to heaven. I no longer believed that my life mattered. I no longer felt that I was worth anything. I believed I made the decision to come to Dubois because I was meant to be forgotten and the people who centered around me were just distractions to boost me up when really it was clear evidence that I had no real future. The awards were all fake. Working so hard to get good grades was a waste of my time. Trying to set an example to my sister and brother by going away to school and doing something with my life had no real purpose. I felt that everything I had experienced leading up to this moment wasn't worth God's time. If someone like Shay could be swept away from this earth so easily and so young, I should just go with the flow and just wait for my time. But I didn't want to wait with God. I didn't want to give myself to someone who could leave me alone in this world like this. I didn't want anything to do with the Lord any longer. Shay was out of my life, and I thought I should just release myself from the Lord as well. With that thought I said my last prayer to the Lord. I asked that He remove the gift of dreams that he gave to me. I asked that He release me of all the warnings in my spirit that I would sometimes get and go out to warn others, because the one warning that cost someone's life, I didn't understand it enough to respond. I told the Lord that I didn't want any gifts, didn't deserve any gifts, and I made a point to add that I was in clear mind while I was asking God of these things. At the end of my prayer I finally felt that I was doing the right thing. God had better things to do, and he had already showed me how my life was going to end up. Without a soul mate!

I didn't feel any different when I woke up that next morning. I thought to myself that it was a process that I had to go through. I was satisfied with being left in this world to walk alone. I didn't expect anyone to really notice the difference in me considering that I wasn't one to reveal these types of situations about myself to others. I thought that as long as I continued to be Leah, I would be okay and to everyone. I continued to do very well in school and even started going out with friends to parties, shopping, and even Clarion University that was just in the next town over. I was smoking often by then. I wasn't really a drinker. I never had been. As a teenager in Germany, us American teens would go out thinking we were grown enough to do what we wanted, and now that it had been years since my first joint, I felt like a pro. I took full advantage of the access I had to pot. I didn't need much to find myself smiling again, but I longed for that feeling. I longed for the feeling of being happy. Looking back, I was in the best situation. I had no children at a young age, able to do anything my heart desired with my life. I had great classmates and friends. I was on my own, but that wasn't enough. No matter what was in my possession, I could not get past that I felt that I had no future. I found myself spending a lot of time in the dorm high. The only time I wasn't smoking was when I was in school and when I went out with friends. My friends smoked, but I wasn't too foolish not to know that I was in an unfamiliar town and not a soul close enough to me if any emergency were to happen. I tried to keep the illegal use of MJ in my dorm where I felt safe enough.

Christmas was growing near and everyone was talking about the plans they had with their families. I was happy that I was going home, but it was bittersweet. I was so excited to see familiar faces; however, I knew that I was going to be very fake about my inner feelings. I wasn't ready to face the reality of everyone's lives, see the couples all around me, and realize that I would never be one of those. I figured that Nanny would be the closest person to feel the way I felt about losing her soulmate. Poppop had passed away almost ten years prior, and if no one else looked like a true couple, my Nanny and Poppop were the two that could set an example of what love is all about. They weren't perfect in my eyes, but they loved each other. Their love encouraged me to desire for a husband in my life, for the rest of my life. Though Poppop was gone, I had not known Nanny to date again. She had a friend but made it very clear to me that he was just a friend and that Poppop was the only man for her. I thought that was who Shay was for me. When Nanny picked me up for the holiday, I wanted to tell her so bad that I was lonely, that I was depressed, that I did nothing but smoke until I could forget. I wanted to beg her to help me, but the words never came out. Four hours of driving, talking, laughing, and it was all fake. Though I wanted to share myself with her, I could not burden Nanny with my problems. I would simply worry her, and who knows what could happen. So, I decided that I would just make the best of the holiday and appreciate the time with her and the family.

I had roughly three weeks off from school. As I approached Bristol, PA, I started to become excited. Though Shay was gone, I had the opportunity to do what I had not done in a while, and that was to spend time with everyone. As a military brat, I did go back to Bristol often; however, it was always with the agenda that I would be leaving to go back to my parents' life. I often felt forced because the life I lived was not my own, and as a child I didn't really enjoy it. Yes, I loved being with my parents, my sister, and brother; however, I longed to be around the entire family. I desired to learn everyone. I was intrigued by the history, the old, the young, the new, and I lacked that my entire life. I was nineteen years old and couldn't name every second cousin I had. I would stand around family and wouldn't recognize them, and that made me so said. I knew that three weeks wouldn't allow me to regain all the missing pieces that I lost in time to have learned as much as I desired to know of my family; however I felt more involved now that my permanent home was finally Bristol. I was so happy to see the cousins and spend time with them all again. As I expected, I received their sympathy for a moment and then life moved on. I was happy that no one dwelled on it because I really didn't want to be put on the spot about Shay. I had enough of my thoughts running through my head, so hearing everyone talking about him would have made it worse. Still, a selfish part of me wanted someone to push more into nosiness just so that I could have a reason to yell and scream out loud as I did inside.

My Nanny was such an encouraging woman. I hadn't had a license yet, so she got me around when family wasn't able to pick me up. I spent a lot of time with the ones my age, as I did when visiting family as an army brat. We went out, ate, clubbed a little, and just enjoyed one another. It was nice, and at times I forgot the depression that was trying to cling to me. The end of the three weeks was approaching fast, and I started to become anxious about going back. There was so much missing from my life, and I realized that I couldn't bear another heartbreak stuck alone. I was in my last week in Bristol but didn't want to go anywhere. I didn't want to hang out any longer. I didn't want to even go to the store with Nanny. I hadn't packed for my return to Dubois and had no real intentions on returning. I didn't want to alarm Nanny, so I would just tell her that I was tired or wasn't feeling well when she asked if I was okay. She asked me to ride with her everywhere that week, and I felt it was much more often than she had done before. Maybe she sensed my nervousness and tried to break me out of it by just getting me in the car. Maybe she had planned to just take me back without my permission if I got in the car. I decided right then that I wasn't going back and no one, not even Nanny, was going to make me go.

One evening when there were just a few days before my date of return, Nanny asked me what was wrong. At that very moment I broke down with all that was inside me. I told her that I couldn't go back, that it was too much, I couldn't do it any more, I missed my family, I wanted to go back to Germany, I missed Shay, and I didn't want to be alone any longer. I just cried as she held me in her arms sharing tears with me. "Oh, baby," she said so softly. "It is going to be okay." Her crying made me feel worse. I didn't want her affected by my confusion. She told me that I had to go back because I had to finish what I started, but if I needed a few days to take some extra days. She then had me call my parents and just talk to them, but that made me feel worse. Again, I was stuck in a position that I didn't want to be in, but this time it was my life choices that placed me here. No one picked Dubois but me! Still I took the couple of days and returned over a week late to school. It wasn't difficult to make up the clock hours or the lessons, but it was a harder pill to swallow to see Nanny leave me again, alone. I took another few days in my dorm without returning to school just to get myself back together. When I did return to class, I was welcomed, and I did my best to place my mind where it needed to be to focus on my life and my future.

The last semester was filled with surprise in my life. I had graduated from my first year of Cosmetology school and passed my state boards to receive my license. I hadn't planned to return to Dubois to finish my manager and instructor license, but when I accomplished the first goal, it made the second and third easier. I also noticed that many of the family I was close to were moving on with their own lives as well, and we were going in separate directions. Even friends were getting pregnant earlier in their lives. Not many of us chose to go to school, but I didn't want to be around those who had boyfriends and children. It reminded me of the life I wouldn't have. I decided that if I was going to be alone, if God had this plan for me, I needed to give it my all and deal with the hand that was chosen for me. I was not in a steady relationship with God and had no intentions on returning; however, I recognized my life and the direction it was going. I was still able be great and do great things. The house, home, family, husband, and kids were behind me, but I could possibly be a traveling lady going from state to state and country to country doing hair, competitions, and maybe even become so big that I could do the hair of stars. Who knows! Whatever it was, I wasn't going to just give up, so I pushed forward.

I still remained within myself never discussing my real feelings and needs to others. I still kept the hurt and pain to myself and focused on others more. I faked as much as possible to try to stay the Leah I was, but I was long from the Leah I knew. I didn't know myself anymore and one of the only things I really had that was still Leah was hair, so I kept that close to me for memory of how happy I really was in my past before life caught up. In hair I felt alive, so I ran with it because it was the only thing I had left. There was a reason that I choose Dubois, so when the summer was over, I made plans to return and finish what I started.

CHAPTER 3

The Wilderness

Titus 1:15 (NKJV)

"To the pure all things are pure, but to those who are defiled and unbelieving nothing is pure; but even their mind and conscience are defiled."

I felt like a widow who had yet to get over the death of my husband, who left me for an eternal life that could have waited for just one lifetime! If Peter said that one day is like a thousand years to the Lord, why couldn't he wait a few thousand for Shay and me to live a once-in-a-lifetime together? I never received those answers, but I was determined not to put my trust in the Lord again until he answered them.

It was a year since Shay's death, and though I wasn't fully healed from it, I found myself surprisingly surviving. I went back to see friends and family in Germany, and it was a little sad. I was scared to place myself back into similar surroundings where Shay and I spent our time, but after getting there, I was fine. Hanging out with friends, spending time with my siblings, and finally having another gyro that I so desperately missed while in America was enough to satisfy me. My friends and I spoke about Shay a few times, and I had the opportunity to see one of his best friends while passing around Baumholder. We spoke a little about Shay, but I dared not to explain my last year. I was stuck in a whirlwind of lies to those around and myself claiming to be alright. I started to believe the coverup story myself. I was still mad at God, but not really focused on Him any longer. I was still alive and well and had so much ahead of me. I had this strange desire not to be alone. I wanted to get back into the dating life and even took those few weeks in Germany as an opportunity to find someone new.

While in Germany I met a soldier, Mike. He was such a gentleman! He reminded me of Shay with the way he treated me and interest in getting in good with my parents. I had a very short time to be in Germany, but Mike was searching for the opportunity to have a significant other and wasn't afraid of a long-distance relationship. He was at the end of his tour and was returning back to Georgia by the end of the year and came without children. I didn't want a rebound boyfriend and really didn't want to take advantage of anyone trying to express their feelings for me in vain, so I took our time together as a huge step into opening my heart to someone new.

I really didn't share my loss with Mike. It wasn't his business, and I refused to be haunted by a spirit that wouldn't even fight to stay with me. Mike didn't talk much of religion, so it wasn't anything that I had to explain. I simply enjoyed the relationship ride for that summer. We went out and talked about family back in the states. I only had a few weeks remaining in Germany before I had to return to hair school, but in those few weeks, we decided to make things official and be a couple. He wasn't really my type. He was shorter than my ideal and seemed very soft. I could tell he was a momma's boy; however, he tried really hard to always keep me smiling, and I liked that. I didn't want to get too close, so I made it clear that I wanted to take things slow. Military relationships to me seemed to go very quickly and marriage was almost instant. I wasn't interested in marriage. I just wanted to date and not feel that lonely feeling within me. Going back to hair school and able to call someone my own was nice again.

It was nice to see a few of my friends again who had stayed in Germany. Some of them had some heartache of their own. Trying to be that big sister example that I had been in the past was difficult for me. I didn't feel like an example any longer, but I felt as if my shame would only hinder them from the opportunity to grow and get through the stage in their life they were going through. So, I continued to encourage and counsel as I did in high school. The only difference this time was much of the words I was speaking was not convincing to me anymore. I was no longer encouraging myself with my inspirational speeches. I was simply talking on what I thought they wanted to hear. It seemed to work, and I continued that pace all through the time I was in Germany. When the time had come, and I had to say goodbye, it was different. It was easier than the last with less tears. Everyone had moved on with their lives, and it was time to move on with mine. Mike made me promise to call him when I got off the plane and back to Nanny's. Another nine-hour trip back to Pennsylvania. Another few months in hair school, and I would finally be done and ready to move on to the next stage of my life.

It was so exciting when Mike called me to say that he had come down back to Georgia and wanted me to come and see him. He had bought me two dozen flowers delivered back to back just to tell me that he missed and loved me. "Love," I thought. I didn't remember confirming that with him; however, the thought was nice. I thought the flowers were it, but I had realized that he purchased a round trip ticket to come see him and stay with his family for the weekend. A three-day paid trip to see my man. I was really feeling myself. I had spoken with the parents over the phone, and his daddy asked me what I had done to Mike in that short period of time. I had no clue what he was talking about, but he went on saying that I had done something. That thought stuck in my head as I got on the flight to Georgia. It was nice to see Mike's face again. We exchanged hugs and kisses before I got into the car to receive my country scenic route to his parents' home. He described how he grew up and gave me some details on his family before we drove up to the driveway of their home. It was small but so beautiful and homey. I was welcomed by his family with open arms. They were expecting me and jumped right in to tour me around the house, tell me about their lives, Mike's childhood. They were just so friendly throughout. Nothing like Southern hospitality! I had never experienced it like this, but it was so nice.

Mike's Dad looked just like him, and I could tell where he got his softer demeanor from. It was surprising to have a sister that was welcoming. From some of my experiences in my past, the sisters would be the hardest to get along with, but she seemed to be so sweet. By dinner time, I had gone over my entire life with the family other than Shay's death. By the time we had dessert, they were completely caught up with the entire military upbringing, ten plus different schools before high school graduation, and almost in completion of hair school. I even learned where the local salons were when Mike and I went out just for a drive. The experience was very odd to me. I felt as if I was being nominated into a family. I felt as if there was a different agenda to my visit, and it began to scare me. I asked Mike not to surprise me his parents gave us their bedroom to stay in over the weekend. "Why would your parents give us their custom-built bedroom with the king size bed and jacuzzi only steps away from the bed?" I thought. The room looked like a massive hotel bedroom. To be this traditional family that he spoke about, I was expecting to sleep in separate beds and rooms. I didn't expect to hear that the family was aware of the future that Mike and I had planned and had accepted that. I wasn't aware nor accepting to our planned future because I wasn't part of the planning. I was taken back to have found out that my entire life was planned out by Mike with expectations that we were getting engaged sooner than later. Sooner as in that weekend! I couldn't believe it. It hadn't been a half year, and this man wanted to marry me. That was the funny looks I was getting from the family. The questions about how many children I wanted and where would I like to get married. That was the reason why I felt rushed to learn about the family and for us to get caught up to speed about our families and background. I've taken a ticket thinking I was coming just for a getaway weekend, and instead there was an expectation for me to go home with a ring on my finger.

Most girls in my situation would have been so excited. They would have said yes so quick when they saw their boyfriend fill the bed with rose petals and chocolates. Any other female that longed for a married life like I did would have been floored to have seen a box being given to her with that little diamond inside signifying a lifetime of hope, love, and a promising future. As for me, I longed for it in my past, but by that present time, I felt just as small as that box I was holding in my hand. I felt like that ring would confine me to a lifestyle that was no longer my desire. My soulmate had left this world, and though I was still furious with him, I realized then that my heart still belonged to him. I couldn't just give my heart to another person, and if I did, it would be on my own terms. I couldn't believe that Mike would even put me in the situation that he did. I felt trapped and forced. Sitting in a house filled with only his family, no one to defend my feelings, understand where I was coming from, or pick me up. We hadn't even spoken about marriage until that weekend. "What was he thinking?" I thought. I just looked at him and asked why. Why would he bring me to Georgia without a warning? Why would he put me on the spot to almost force my yes? What if these people were crazy, and if I didn't say yes, I would be cut in a bunch of pieces? I really didn't know what the outcome was going to be, but telling me that you loved me just wasn't enough for me to say yes after three months. It wasn't enough for me. Mike wasn't enough for me. I thought that it might be the only ring I would ever be offered. I thought my saying no was going to negatively affect my entire life, but I couldn't live in a lie and live in it knowing that he loved me, but I didn't love him back. I looked at Mike in his eyes and explained that I just wasn't ready yet, and I couldn't make any promises of when I was going to be ready, but I was willing to see where the relationship went. I could not believe his response. He was such a gentleman to tell me that he understood as tears rolled down my face. He was willing to wait.

I was so fortunate that night as he held me knowing I had just denied him but the guilt inside my spirit was so strong that I couldn't stay. The next morning when I got up, I asked Mike to get me a ticket to go home that day instead of staying the remainder of the weekend. He pleaded with me, but I just couldn't. I couldn't stay there another day knowing that the ring I was offered should have been coming from Shay. I didn't want to stay another day in Mike's family house knowing that my disappointment, shame, and tears were coming to me due to an entirely different situation that they weren't even aware of. I had to get out. I had to get away. The gentlemen that Mike was, I had a ticket by the beginning of the afternoon. I called Nanny to change her plans to come get me from the airport. I hugged Mike's parents and thanked them for their hospitality. Mike's sister finally began to feel like a real sister as she cut her eyes at me when we hugged. I guess she noticed that I wasn't wearing a ring the next morning or Mike might have told her himself. I lied as I told them I hoped to see them again. My heart was telling me that I would never see them again. The hug and kiss that Mike and I shared at the airport was different than the others. I knew it was over then; it would just be a matter of time. As I got on the plane and sat in my seat, I began to cry. I cried because I was embarrassed. I cried because I was only twenty years old but tired of my life already. I cried because I felt God was trying to make up for taking Shay away from me, but I was disappointed in what I thought was God's way to say sorry. So, I took the time on the plane by myself to cry until the pilot said that there was only a short time until we would be landing in Philadelphia. I had to get myself together to see Nanny and act like the trip went well with a slight hiccup. Nanny said she had a feeling that was going to happen and was happy that I trusted my heart when I said no to the proposal.

Mike and I were distant after a few weeks, and when his duty station had changed to Texas, we were over one another. I honestly would have given it some real time and tried to work towards the love that he claimed to have for me, but I think the answer to Mike was final. I felt his lifestyle changing and Southern momma's boy role was changing into that typical soldier mentality. The calls had become less, the conversations short, and the little feelings we had left were becoming nonexistent. The last call was so awkward as we tried to tell one another it just wasn't working out. When I told him that he didn't seem into the relationship any longer, he was contradicting, and as he tried to explain to me that I was distant I did the same. We came to a mutual agreement to just be friends for a while; however, I think we both knew that was the last time we would talk, and it was.

I heard the enemy's voice that my life was going to be like this. Filled with the opportunity to be with people but never satisfied and never desiring of them. Sadly enough, I agreed with the enemy, but I couldn't allow anyone in close enough to tell them that. I walked around with my pride telling the world and myself that I wasn't ready to settle down. Telling the world that people like Mike were crazy to think about wanting to get married so early into a relationship, as if Shay and I were together longer than nine months. As if I wasn't head over hills for Shay almost the moment we began dating and maybe even before that when I saw him walking into my Popeye's to order those shrimp baskets and fries every day. The feelings I thought I suppressed for a lifetime were returning in an instant, and it was harder to hide it this time because I wasn't in my school dorm to hate the world, God, and Shay or smoking my life away. I was now in the presence of my Nanny, and she was too dear to my heart to fill her up with the loneliness I felt inside. My cousins were too dependant on me to be that big sister like example for me to pour my heart out and cry to them. My siblings were too far away for me to send over that spirit of depression from their big sister when I was expected to be going away to show them what we are supposed to do as young adults. And my parents, I felt, more than anyone, because they have been around me for my entire life, should know what was going on inside me. Every time they asked if I was okay, they should have known I wasn't. I forced my tears out. I was confident that God knew; however, I felt that this was His will for me, so asking for a change was irrelevant.

I became a master at hiding how I truly felt. I realized that if I stayed involved in everyone else's life, and if I focused on things outside my own needs, I could forget—or more likely ignore—what was going on with me. If my only personal focus was going to school and finishing, I would be good. I had that going for me, and my mind was still focused on ensuring that hair remained my strength. Back in school, I had the opportunity to see some old classmates. A few of us, some new, decided to go into the instructor's program that year, and we were a very strong class. The knowledge and the desire made me feel almost as good as I did my senior year when I knew where I was going and what I was doing with my life. It was easy to jump right into my responsibilities for the best grades, and there was even an expectation at the school for me to be one of the best. I set my bar high with my teachers the year before, and I was still trying to keep communication with my cosmetology teacher in Baumholder, Germany, so the pressure was on to do great things.

I took a job about a block from my school with an Italian lady in her fifties. She had been in Dubois since she was young. Our interview was good. I've been told that I interview well, I think, mainly because I didn't really go for jobs that I wasn't interested in, so I was very passionate in explaining why I wanted to be part of the team. As for Lucy, I told her that I was looking for work, had raw talent in doing hair and have been styling hair for years. I also explained that I needed the experience with different hair types, which was one of the main reasons I had chosen to move to Dubois in the first place. I became the shampoo lady, which was an upgrade from the salon cleaner position, which was an upgrade from the usual first job of a mom and pop salon, so I felt privileged. So, every day after school, I had a job that kept me occupied, out of trouble, practicing my trade, and away from the drinking and marijuana until night time. I began to appreciate Lucy's wisdom as well. She was older and didn't seem to have that odd, indirect prejudice that I had to ignore in the mostly white town of Dubois. It wasn't overly offensive. I didn't have to worry about cops stopping me or getting those odd looks in the local mall, but every now and then I would get some nappy head comment from the more seasoned ladies getting their hair done. It was funny how they wouldn't hesitate to tell me that they didn't want those "tighter curls with the blue rods," and then end the statement with, "I know YOU know what I mean!" It took me half of my first year and some very defensive white friends from the town always wanting to defend me to find out what they truly meant. I would also get comments on my complexion. A little lighter than their expectation of a black girl, I guess! I was always told I had olive skin, not brown skin. I was always questioned if I was mixed with something and the answer was always no. Lucy, on the other hand, would tell me the most interesting stories of how when she moved to Dubois when there were no blacks in the town, and Italians were the minority. She described the harshness that she had to endure and how strong she remained in the midst of supporting her husband's move to the town. She got her license, made a name for herself, purchased her home and the house on the right next to her to build her salon. At the time she was hiring me, she was purchasing the house on the other side of her home for the spa she was building. A business woman who fought her way against all odds! I was impressed and motivated to be around such wisdom. Lucy made me feel stronger and able to get through the hard times when I wanted to give up. She really didn't know my story, but hers was enough not to feel sorry for myself all the time.

School was much shorter then. The manager and instructor's license were only a few hundred clock hours totaling about six months. Easy breezy for me. I continued school. Working for Lucy, however, I made some new friends from class. These friends were from the Clarion area, which was next to the closest college, Clarion University. College life was much different than my away-from-home experience. I thought I was out and free in Dubois but realized that college opened up so many more opportunities to dominantly be around my own age group. When I would go to my friends' homes in Clarion, I was no longer in the mix of my generation trying to find their way and an older wiser group that has made it through some things and finally decided to get themselves together like in Dubois. In Clarion, my peers were mostly my age and the ones who were older didn't act like it or you wouldn't know. Dubois had the lifestyle of family, finding a husband, making a life, having children, and getting a career. Clarion was more of the opportunity to get out into the world, taking advantage of a carefree lifestyle before stepping into adulthood of responsibility. More parties, more alcohol, more marijuana, and many ways to act a fool. Quickly, I found it the place I wanted to be. There were areas and people that could have been considered responsible and mature, however I couldn't say I knew that type. I felt more free and seemed to have less anxiety and worry about my future without Shay, so I jumped right in.

I wasn't really too much of a fan of the American marijuana. It always seemed to make me sick or more paranoid than in Germany. Still it did the job of hiding all the pain I felt inside. It made me feel alive in my darkness, and I was much livelier with much more smiles high or drunk. My intoxication of choice had always been marijuana. Alcohol was just the legal stuff for me since I had made it to my twenty-first birthday the summer before. When I couldn't get to the MJ, I would deal with the alcohol. Clarion was filled with a life I had not too much been exposed to. I had the parties back in Germany. I also went to clubs as a teenager; however, the atmosphere was much different. Baumholder seemed to be filled more with a maturity level that was very unfamiliar in Clarion. I'm sure there were the ones that had their head on straight and knew what they were doing and where they were going with their life; however, the crowd I was around really didn't have much direction than get high and party, and it was right up my alley. I had an even share of friends who were college students and others who were workers, but none of them lacked the ability to have a good time.

It was okay to be careless in Clarion, and I made the decision to find the opportunity to move to Clarion. For a while I had stayed with some friends, and with the car my parents had bought me, I was able to travel between Dubois and Clarion with ease to stay working for Lucy. By the time I had graduated from my final program in hair school, I already had a roommate to move into a trailer apartment with in Clarion to be more independent and had found a salon to work at in Clarion. I left Lucy and was promoted to a hair dresser at my new job after a few weeks of washing hair. I checked on Lucy a few times, but in young adult age, checking on people who cared for you at least four to five times is enough so the drives to Dubois became less, and eventually I didn't communicate with her any longer.

Living in Clarion was different than visiting and going to the local bar to hang out with friends. I found that the level of prejudice was much more expressed in Clarion; however, the diversity was much higher. Oddly enough, it felt more like back home in Bristol where my family grew up. It wasn't always about color but about who you knew. The better the last name, the better the outcome of every situation. I didn't live in Bristol much to have those experiences; however, going to a few schools and almost getting some driving tickets in Bristol helped me to open my eyes to my last name advantage. Clarion seemed to be the same. If you were involved with the right people, you were okay. I was privileged to be around the right people, I guess! From drug dealers, shop owners, strippers, Clarion born and raised kids to even professors, I found out very quickly that people were getting to know me just enough for me to be comfortable in most areas. It made it easier to have a boldness when I would get stopped late at night coming home from the bar, drunk out of my mind and trying to drive steady down the single street two miles to my home. Getting stopped seemed to be more of a hobby for the officers than a discipline for me. They would walk up slowly and then look at my face and ask what I was doing out so late. They knew exactly what bar I was coming from; however, I was always respectful and responded well and as truthful as I could.

I must have been issued fifty warnings by the same two cops before getting tired of clubbing at the local bar and just enjoying my levels of intoxication at home or my friend's homes. It was safer anyway because we began to hear about all the high-level drug busts going on around Clarion. There were also kids being forced into getting involved when getting caught selling or using on campus, questioned by law enforcement, then forced to make the decision to talk or lose their opportunity to finish school. Some were even threatened to lose their scholarships. It was sad, and for the first time in a long time I was very scared of that being involved. I wasn't in college, just a working girl now living in a town; however, I didn't want to become a statistic to the world. Just another girl getting wrapped up in the wrong thing and finding herself caught up. I stayed low, especially considering I now had a roommate that was very much involved in the drug world and able to keep himself on the low. I didn't know how he did it, but I felt very protected just because of the people I was around. It was so careless; however, I was grown and doing my thing as an adult.

Deuteronomy 11: 16 (NKJV)

"Take heed to yourselves, lest your heart be deceived, and you turn aside and serve other gods and worship them,"

Though it was an ordinary lifestyle for a twenty-two-year-old girl, I was fortunate to have what I did. My boss was very cool and very well known in Clarion. She had done well for herself and picked up a lot of clientele in the area. She had the locals and the advantage of the college. I wasn't a star in the town but once again found myself like in DuBois with an understanding to ethnic hair, allowing me to pick up the clients that didn't want to travel all the way to Pittsburgh just to get their hair done. I wasn't doing many extensions; however, the colors, simple wash and style, and my personal favorite, updos, kept me happy. One day I came into the shop and my boss told me that a man was looking for me about his hair. She explained that he was in theater and looking for some work for a production that was going on at the college. She mentioned to me that I would need to commit a few weeks to the processes it was going to take to transform him into the character that he needed to be for the play. I had a consultation with him that afternoon, and as soon as she told me, I felt so honored. Who is this person? Was it because my older cousin worked at the college, and he found that I was related? I had two employees from the college who came to me that way, so it wouldn't have been a surprise. Still, I couldn't stop looking at the front door, waiting for the time to come when he walked through that door. "Wow," I thought. To be in my first year in this town and being considered for the opportunity to do hair for a major production like a college musical had my stomach twisting up. I had no other information to go on, and right before I couldn't stand the anxiousness any longer, he walked through the door. He was a taller gentleman and looked very calm and cool. He went to the desk, and though I couldn't hear him, I'm sure he asked for my name. He sat in the chair because I was finishing a client's hair at the time. He waited patiently for me; however, not too long.

Once completed, I sat down in the front with the man, who I found out was one of the theater professors playing one of the main characters of the play. He mentioned that the transformation was going to be very dramatic because his character forced him to completely change his look. When he showed me the picture of Riff Raff, I was almost taken back. When he said dramatic, he was under exaggerating. The transformation was almost unconvincing. He had the height and the long face; however, the baldness at the top, the stringy, thin hair, and more importantly, going from very dark brown to that drastic blond without extensions didn't look possible. For some reason, he had the confidence in me to do it, and with his confidence, I swallowed the doubt within me and simply said yes. He asked me if I knew anything about The Rocky Horror Picture Show, which was the play they were putting on in a few weeks. I told him that I had no idea what it was about, so he told me to look it up. We went over the time it was going to take to complete the transformation, the extensions that were needed, and the cost. There was nothing that we spoke about that intrigued me more than what he was about to pay me to do this work. I couldn't believe it was going to be well into the hundreds just for a few hours of a process and upkeep for the five-day production. I went home so excited that day, and I was on high.

When the day had come to begin the begin the process of his transformation, he had cameras for before and after shots and really set this glamorous picture of the life of theater. He was very quiet most of the time during the first stages and almost as if he was studying, taking pictures throughout. He was persistent about staying in the front of the mirror during the process to watch as his hair went through all the stages to lift his dark hair to this almost dying, stringing light-yellow tint. I cut into his hair to make it even thinner. The process was tedious as we bleached, washed, conditioned, and bleached again. When we were half way through the coloring process, he asked me if I had the opportunity to look up the play. I was too embarrassed to admit that I really didn't bother to look up the play and simply took the pictures of the characters that he had given me from the consultation. I studied the techniques I was going to use to lift his hair to such a light color without losing all the hair on his head so I could braid a few pieces of it to add the weave. So, I lied and said that looked it up. He got so excited that I took the time to look up the play and still had a smile on my face, but I wasn't sure why. He started talking about the play a little discretely; however, I wasn't sure what the secret was. He asked me about parts that I had absolutely no idea what he was talking about; however, I nodded my head and made sure to smile and laugh when he did to show my continued fake interest. He went on through the end of the process; however, through all his talking I still really didn't know what this picture was about. The only thing on my mind was that I felt like a stylist for a movie star. He had come later in the afternoon and the process was so long that it took us into the later evening hours. It was only the theater professor, my boss, and I by the time I finished. He allowed me to turn him away from the mirror as I added the extensions. I wanted at least the finished product to be a surprise, and after confirming that the color was equivalent to what we were trying to achieve, he allowed me to finish with his back to the mirror.

It felt like such an accomplishment to see his face light up when I finally turned the chair around to take his first look in his character. He was completely satisfied and kept thanking and hugging me. I told him it wasn't a problem at all and thanked him for the opportunity to be a part of his play behind the scenes. He gave me tickets and thanked my boss for suggesting that I would be the one for the job. He made me promise to try to attend; however, I knew that I was scheduled to work each day of the play. I took the tickets anyway and took my big check. That night I went home. I felt bad about not really having interest in the play enough to look it up before. Though I was told I did a good job, as usual, I critiqued myself on all the things I could have done better. In the event I am approached again with the same scenario or even a bigger opportunity there were a few things I definitely could have improved on, but the one that stuck to me was getting in character with the character. How could I have really done justice and the best job that I could if I had no idea of the character I was creating. I wasn't the one on stage; however, I was a part of creating the character, and to do that successfully I should have started to become the character with him. So even though it was after the fact, I decided to look up The Rocky Horror Picture Show. To my surprise it was all about a topic that I was not at all familiar with. Though set up more like the Frankenstein picture, to my understanding the main point was the transformation of lifestyles. Prior to that moment, I had not known anything nor really been exposed much to the LGBT lifestyle and had no real opinion of it because I wasn't involved. Still, I lost interest in going further into the plot of the play and was a little relieved that I was working all the nights of the play, so I had a real excuse not to go and didn't have to lie when the professor returned the following week to thank me as he had his extensions removed and color put back as best as we could. He said it was a success, and I was happy for him.

CHAPTER 4

The Hook

1 John 2:15-16 (NKJV)

"Do not love the world or the things in the world. If anyone loves the world, the love of the Father is not in him. For all that is in the world – the lust of the flesh, the lust of the eyes, and the pride of life – is not of the Father but is of the world."

After a few months in Clarion I became interested in the campus. I was getting bored with the normal routine of work and home. So many people around me my age were so involved with all the college activities and after getting over the partying and recreational drugs, I wanted to discover other opportunities outside of my boring routine. I was still young, in my early twenties, and though I had not decided to continue pursuing school, I still had the desire to be involved with what young adults my age were doing. In the area there wasn't much to do but hang out at someone's house or try to be more active on campus. I wasn't in college, so I was very limited to campus life; however, it didn't stop me from wanting it. My roommate had invited me to a basketball game at the school, and I was so excited to go. The men's game was so lively, and I was so excited to be a part of it. It felt almost like I was back in Baumholder as a teenager with many hats. I went to school and worked back then, but I was also a cheerleader and a captain by my senior year. The memories of traveling game to game and all the chants and cheers came back as if they never left me. I sat in the bleachers, not really knowing a single player; however, I just replaced their faces and jersey numbers with the players from my old high school. I watched the cheerleaders as they cheered and did half time. I got involved with all the remarks when the team would score. It was altogether a great time and became my pastime. The girls' basketball team would always follow the guys, and I would stay when I had nothing else to do. It was just as interesting to watch, but not as lively. The hate I had for Shay leaving me was finally subsiding, and I felt as if I was really getting over him. I wasn't dating anyone and had no real interest in dating for a while but felt the spirit I had kept so dear to be angry leave me, and I was happy to be growing up.

Like a well-rounded sports fan, the game became my hobby. Even without my roommate, I was going to the games and staying both games. I was approached a few times by some guys but didn't feel that instant spark and so ignored the stares and comments. Many of them actually looked like a bunch of babies from where I was standing. I was their age but working and had an apartment and responsibilities of my own. No classes to go to the following day with ready paid-for meals three times a day by the scholarships or mommy and daddy. I didn't have the luxury to take an extra four to five years to grow up and for some reason every time I would see a guy making a pass at me, their lack of independence was a setback in my eyes. With that thought consistently in my head, I couldn't move past it enough just to even smile back at them and was almost scared of being approached for my number or a date. Instead I took interest to a girl on the team. I remembered her face from the bar that I would go to. She didn't really dance much and for some reason her face was so welcoming, almost familiar, but I knew I had not met her in the past. Tay was her name. She was on the girls' team and pretty good. She had that wannabe thug look to her, and even though it seemed obvious what she was down with, I didn't want to judge. When we walked past one another while walking out of the gym, we introduced ourselves, and I told her that I remembered her from the bar. She remembered as well and also noticed she didn't see me around the campus much. I explained that I lived in Clarion and was not going to school but working. I told her good game, and we exchanged numbers to hang out. I was honestly relieved! I had not met a new person in about six months. I loved my friends, but the same routine consumed us, and I was dying for something or someone new.

I few days later I saw Tay walking as I was driving past the campus and stopped to say hi. She was on her way home, so I gave her a ride, and in return she invited me up to her apartment. When I walked in, it was then I had no doubt in my mind that everyone in Clarion did some type of drug and had no problem openly expressing themselves in an intoxicating way. I could have been anyone, but that didn't stop Tay from rolling up, lighting up, and offering me a hit. I was more than willing to indulge in the carelessness, and so we became more acquainted with one another freely about our current lives. She was going to school for psychology, which struck my interest immediately because it was a major that I personally was so much attracted to. I always told myself that if I was blessed to be smarter and had the finances, I would have been a psychologist or a doctor. Though Ty wasn't from the local area, she wasn't far from home. She lived near Pittsburgh, which struck my interest again because many of my family members were from that area. Not many that I personally knew, but I knew where the family came from.

Nothing in the apartment/dorm seemed out of order and Ty seemed like a very nice person. I didn't want to judge but really found no other understanding as to the choice of boyish clothes she chose to wear; however, I did associate her with the tomboy look that I had been exposed to while in high school. Many of our girls from the basketball team of my school had that same boyish demeanor; however, their attire wasn't so hard. More like a T-Boz or Left Eye look from the TLC group, (boyish on a cute girly level). Ty's look was much harder and after a few more puffs into a deeper intoxication level, I found out from her girlfriend, who walked in and introduced herself, exactly what I noticed to be different. There was no longer any need to judge as they gave each other a kiss and hug, asked each other how their day was, and then sat next to each other as a couple would commonly do. I tried to look normal as I was standing witness to this type of exposure. Inside myself I knew I didn't look a bit normal or comfortable. I had never seen the same sex in action as a couple before, and if I had not been in a different mindset, I might have run right out of there, but I didn't. Instead, I forced myself to become open to their personal choice and indulge a little longer in their company and left in enough time to get home to get ready for work the next day. Me being the over-analyzer, I had not figured out why I was placed in their particular situation and kept searching for an answer as I drove home. Their open relationship was on my mind all night to the point that I didn't get that much sleep. They looked so comfortable and even happy, but they had to know that wasn't the way!

A few days had gone past and I had not heard from Ty, but she was on my mind. I gave her a call just to say hi, but she didn't pick up, so I left a message. She called back later in the day sounding as if she was relaxing. She invited me over and so I obliged. When I got over there the smoke was so heavy. I asked about the fear of random drug tests or exposure considering she was going to school on a basketball scholarship, but she didn't seem to care about any of that. Maybe she knew when it occurred and simply stopped or had something that disguised it. Whatever it was, there was no fear in Ty. We continued our conversation about our lives and ultimately led to her choice to be with women and my choice to be with no one. Her answer seemed so sure that it almost encouraged me. Inside myself, I felt she knew it wasn't the right choice, but she didn't seem to think that way. She just spoke about what made her happy, and that was what women did for her. I never heard her talk badly about men, she simply chose females. I, on the other hand, had a much different response to the same question. I was much more confused with my decision to be alone. I spoke about the tragedy with Shay and how I lost myself in his death. I explained how I just can't seem to find comfort thinking about being with men any longer. There was so much that I mentally invested in with Shay and knew that he was who I was supposed to be with. Now that it was no longer possible, all other men simply didn't add up to what Shay and I should have had. Ty immediately sympathized and comforted me, then responded with a suggestion to try something new. We looked at each other and began to laugh as she told me she was only playing, but I didn't really feel she was playing at all. I asked about her girlfriend and she explained that they had been together for a while. That she can be jealous one, but she gets over it. We spoke more about our lives and my level of comfort continued to grow. After a few weeks Ty and I were inseparable, and I saw less of her girlfriend but was not alarmed because they had different schedules.

Sometime had passed when I saw Ty with another friend. This one was a guy, stocky from afar, and when I approached him to be introduced, and he seemed to play football, but he looked so familiar. Ty was with her girlfriend, who I had not seen in a while. She was so excited to introduce me to Ty's friend. We exchanged names, and I told Mickey that he looked so familiar. Ty had this big smile on her face as if she knew something but didn't say much. He looked a little funny to me, but I was over my past ways of only finding interest in what I would say is good looking. I just wanted to meet people and just be free of all the limits, rules, and stipulations that I put on myself throughout my life. I was being exposed to people who seemed to be living lives that were happier. I saw more smiles, heard less worries, and also saw that what they spoke about doing in their lives was actually happening instead of just words. I didn't find Mickey to be very attractive, but who was I to say so? I wasn't looking for a boyfriend but to get to know people.

Mickey seemed shy and without any interest of his own to hook up, so it made the conversation easier. I couldn't help but notice the largeness of his chest for a man. It was so odd as if Mickey was reading my mind because he began to explain that Ty and he grew up together and played ball together in high school. He said that they choose different schools to go to, but they have been best friends for a while. That's when I figured out that Mickey's chest area was actually women's breasts. Mickey was a girl! I was completely in shock because I had not picked that up at all. It was amazing to me that Mickey was so persistent on explaining her sex as if she knew there was sometimes a confusion. I became more interested in the idea of befriending Mickey, now exposed to her honestly. There was a humbleness about her that could not be overlooked, as well as a welcoming spirit with most inviting eyes. We exchanged numbers before they left.

The first few phone calls were so uncomfortable. Not for Mickey, I'm sure; however, I didn't feel like I was talking to a friend like Ty. It felt completely different, and I found myself feeling as if I was back in high school getting to know a guy that I had warm feelings for. I was very much aware of who Mickey was, which made it even more odd considering my past was never consumed with the confusing thoughts and feelings that were beginning to take over my spirit. I played cool and felt almost relieved because though my feelings were completely out of place at the time, Mickey had a girlfriend, and I was never one to play the other woman or have a person on the side, so the friendship we were building felt genuine and without an agenda. I also felt protected from my feelings because

Mickey went to school in Chicago. The farther the better so that whatever I was going through stayed locked away in my thoughts.

From the late night talks I found out that Mickey had a rough upbringing. She was raised by her mom and step-father who was around most of her life. Her grandmother didn't live very far away, and she was very close to her. Mickey was very close to her stepfather until being mo-lested as a child, which lasted well into her teenage years. When she finally got the nerve to expose the truth to her mother, she was cast out, as if not the first born, and forced to live with her grandmother for a period of time. Bas-ketball seemed to be Mickey's outlet, and she did it very well, allowing her personal life to be well hidden from the public. Summers were easy to stay away with camps, and there was not a doubt being one of the best ball players of her area in that time that college was a definite. She knew she had a bright future, and for that she kept whatev-er relationship she could come from a mother not believing her daughter. She loved her mother but simply felt that her mother loved her stepfather more and was not willing to live a single life for a daughter exposing such a horren-dous act after so long of tolerating it. Mickey felt as if her mother took the molestation more as a relationship that came from adolescent years when a young lady begins to get those type of feelings. Her mother was convinced that if the accusations were true, Mickey wanted it and just be-came upset with her stepfather and tried to break up a life that had been building since Mickey was a smaller child. Whatever the reason, at the time Mickey was telling me her past, I could still hear the pain in her story though she claimed to have been over it.

When Mickey returned from school we decided to go out. She knew of a little place close to where she lived, so I took the forty-five-minute drive west to scoop her up and go out. It was a little hole-in-the-wall bar, lightly filled with some locals who had known Mickey for a long time. They confirmed the warm, genuine spirit that I picked up immediately when we met and was excited that she had moved with another woman. We both very quickly denied any relationship or future opportunities claiming each other as only friends. That's the first time that I heard Mickey say that I was not in that life. I wasn't sure where that came from; however, I just kept quiet and offered a smile to Mickey's best friend since childhood. Jeff knew Mickey basically all their life. Shockingly, he was a man, and that is exactly what Mickey asked me when she noticed my facial reaction when I found her best friend to be a guy. They talked about how they even had a crush on each other growing up; however, it just didn't work out that way. I asked Jeff if he was in the life, and he gladly responded with a no. He explained that he was truly convinced Mickey was really going to stay in the life, but there was no doubt in my mind that if anyone would stay in such a lifestyle Mickey would be it. There was not a feminine trait in her that I could see, and she had adapted the male habits so well that I couldn't see anyone who would think anything different. We stayed out late that night, so I was invited to stay out in her area at her parents' house. I felt a little weird staying under a roof that felt like it was so filled with confusion; however, I was tired and intoxicated and not really interested in driving back home and taking a chance of getting stopped, so I stayed. We entered the house so late that everyone was sleep. Mickey went into her parents' house to explain the situation, and we went to her room and talked until we both passed out.

I woke up to find myself in bed alone. I wasn't sure where Mickey had gone and scared to leave the room, I just waited, smelling the breakfast cooking until her return. Who I had expected to be her stepfather walked in unannounced; however, I wasn't surprised! In my parents' home there was no privacy regardless of the kids' age, so other than being nervous to meet the monster that I heard so much about, I was okay. I found my spirit relieved to see Mickey come right in the door after her stepfather took a few steps in to introduce himself. She introduced us, and I gave the best greeting I could and forced my feelings to stay within myself. He seemed very nice, and I figured if Mickey could be cordial, I had to oblige myself being a guest. When he left the room, Mickey asked how I slept and handed me a washcloth while directing me to the bathroom.

As I washed up, my stomach felt as if I was carrying a fifty-pound weight. I didn't understand what was happening to me and though most of it felt odd, I wasn't feeling as I had in the past about homosexuality. It was obvious to me why Mickey was in the lifestyle. She had been hurt, mistreated, abused, misunderstood, and cast out by the closest people in her life. My emotions began to build up inside myself with the hurt and pain of anyone mistreated and misunderstood. Still I kept my composure as I walked back into Mickey's room to get ready to join her down in the kitchen for breakfast. I found myself focusing on how I was going to introduce myself as if I had the need to impress her parents when I really wanted to be old enough to go off on them both. Instead, I found myself sitting at the table being properly introduced to Mickey's mother, stepfather, and little brother who was so cute. We ate and I got to know a little more about the star player of her time, while the family learned of my army brat life with my parents. It ended up being a very good breakfast. Mickey's mother was very nice. Still I couldn't get past what I had heard about her, but I could never disrespect anyone's parents, and Mickey still treated her like a queen. As we said our goodbyes and left the house, Mickey's mother invited me back any time, and I thanked her for the hospitality. She told Mickey that I had a good head on my shoulders.

Mickey and I decided to spend the day together, so I called off work and just hung out around the town. I was very interested to know how she could still be so close to her parents after such an experience, but Mickey continued to say she was over it. She simply made the decision that she was either going to stay stuck in a world of hatred or simply forgive them for what she had to experience and love them for what they had done right. I just couldn't believe it and found myself so ashamed of who I was. If anyone did anything wrong to me, I wasn't a fighter; however, I stayed as far away from that person as I could. I didn't see myself so easily to forgive or find myself smiling and having a life in such mess, but to be judging Mickey's situation wasn't right either. She had her reasons. Can you really be upset with your mother for life, I thought? Even with her stepfather's situation, he did help to raise her most of her life, and she had developed father-like feelings for him through all of that. She wasn't going to be the reason for her little brother to be raised without a father, which is what would have happened if Mickey pursued any further about her being molested. Still I could not agree with one person having to deal with the weight of the world on one's own when the causes were not her decision. My heart melted as Mickey continued to share with me more of her past, and after I opened up to her with my last year and a half without Shay, Mickey seemed to look at me as if a light bulb popped up in her head. I asked her what she was thinking about, but she wouldn't say. She just said she understands. The conversation seemed to shift into the lifestyle. I asked Mickey if her past is what got her to where she was in her life with women. Mickey explained that the only man she could have seen herself with was her best friend, and they were too much like brother and sister to even think about anything like that; however, they made a promise to have a baby together if neither of them got married. I laughed because that was exactly what my ex and I promised one another as well when we were young. I guess that need for security stretches no matter who you are.

As the time went from morning to afternoon, Mickey and I had already drove around the small town, walked a little, met up with her best friend, smoked a little and found ourselves back in the car just sitting and talking. I was main topic at this point as to my experience with females. I explained to Mickey I really had none and wasn't even raised where the topic came up. I had always been the type that knew that I would have a husband, children, and career but was taken back once Shay left me. Mickey reminded me that it wasn't Shay's choice to leave, but I wasn't trying to hear that. Psychologically, I was convinced that if Shay loved me enough, he would have fought harder. Mickey didn't agree! I was almost angry to hear her defend Shay's death as if she knew him. I explained that since then I just can't see myself with another man. I tried to date after him and it didn't work out. I even tried to go back to my past relationship and found myself lost in it. I told her that I was not meant to be with men. "So, you're meant to be with women,?" Mickey asked.

It was the first time she had asked that question and the first time I really had to think about it. Until then I didn't see myself pursuing females; however, I wasn't making any attempt to date men any longer. I told her that I was open for whatever, but I was sure that my soul mate was long gone from this world, and as long as I remained in this world, I was sure I wouldn't be with a man again. Mickey explained that if I went around talking like that to other lesbians they would take full advantage of my statement and emotions. I asked for understanding and listened as she explained that the lifestyle is no different than the relationships that I was used to; however, I sounded as if I was a lost puppy emotionally, and that is easy game to take advantage of anyone, no matter what the sexual preference. She was sure to add that I was not gay! I realized that Mickey had been saying that a lot, so I asked if she was trying to convince me or herself of my sexuality. She was confident that I was going through a lot but when I came out of it, I would be back to the life I have known and loved. She made a statement that she was willing to be there with me as I went through what I did, as if she was doing me a favor. I wasn't so much an emotional wreck to have not picked up that cheap line of desperation, so I got angry with Mickey. I explained to her that even though I was hurt, I wasn't stupid. It was clear that she had feelings for me, and I wasn't about to be used as if my pain was going to be the excuse as to us getting together like she was saving me from destruction. I began to cry but couldn't figure out why. I felt like I was having an argument with a significant other that was not understanding to my feelings. Mickey grabbed ahold of me and hugged me tight as she apologized repeatedly for making me cry. As I hugged her back, it felt good to just be held again by someone I felt really meant it. Not hugging me for something, or because they know they did me wrong or felt pity for me, but simply because I needed the hug at the time. When we realized that the hug was lasting so long, we both oddly stood back from each other, gave a weird smile at one another, and made the decision that it was getting late. I dropped Mickey back off at home and went on my way back to Clarion. I got a little lost on the way but made it back home. I called Mickey to let her know I was safe; and we talked some more until we both got too tired to stay on the phone. We both agreed that we had a great time and promised to talk more often and see each other until Mickey returned to school.

The phone conversations and visits became more and more frequent as Mickey and I got better acquainted with one another. It was nice to have someone in my life again that I could talk to about anything and who could open up to me. It was like we were each other's motivator. I wasn't sure about Mickey, but I needed her in my life more than ever. I felt as if the pain of the memories wasn't there when I was around her. I became dependent on our phone time since Mickey was much farther from me after her return to school. I had not gone out to her school to visit her and wasn't sure if I would be putting on a true face by taking the energy and money going all the way out to Chicago to see her. "What message would that give?" I thought, and so the phone seemed more appropriate. Still I missed Mickey greatly and found myself showing odd signs of interest in her, and I was so happy that it was not as easily seen over the phone. I missed her and didn't want to get off the phone most of the time. We found ourselves falling asleep on the phone and one of us waking the other up just to say good night.

I even found myself calling more often in the daytime just to say hi and see how she was doing, until one day I told her that I missed her. There was dead silence after my statement and then Mickey replied with the same response that she missed me as well. My heart started beating really fast, and I couldn't find the words to say. I hurried off the phone and said that I would talk to her later not knowing what feelings I was having at that moment. When I got off the phone, I was very aware of the statement I had made and found myself so confused in my thoughts and feelings. I ignored the rings as Mickey made a few attempts to call me back that evening. I couldn't answer. I had nothing to say, wasn't sure of my feelings, and scared of what was going on inside of me. So, I decided to do what any normal young scared girl would do in this situation and just ignore my comment as if it never happened.

"It was a simple statement," I thought as I looked at my phone for the next couple of days without any contact with Mickey. I knew that many people say they miss you as friends, family, and loved ones without making a big deal out of it, but to me this was different. Mickey wasn't just a friend, but a female in the life! A life that I had no interest in as a child or growing up. A lifestyle that I never seen myself participating in, and now with all this exposure to this lifestyle, I was becoming more accepting of the possibility that I had been wrong about my belief in the life. I was beginning to wonder if I could possibly find happiness in such a life if I would only try. The thoughts filtering through my mind seemed scary to me, and I couldn't speak to Mickey with all the confusion. Almost a week had gone by, and I started feeling like a horrible friend for not offering an excuse for such a change in our routine. I decided to woman up and call her; however, found myself speaking to an answering machine and not just once, a few times.

Now a week of not hearing each other's voice, and it was official we were on a different level without phone relationship. Both mad at one another; Mickey mad at me for not calling her back after her many calls of concerns and myself mad at Mickey for not returning my calls after I got up the nerve to call her back. By the time we did speak the both of us were going back and forth as a couple how we needed to release some stress, which made everything even more confusing. I decided to be honest with Mickey and tell her that my feelings were changing, and I wasn't sure what was going on, but I had to be open with her about them. When asked to be more specific about my feelings, I explained that I was beginning to like Mickey more than just a friend. She was already very much aware of my lack of experience from my past in the life and explained to me that the feelings could simply be coming from my own personal need for a companion. I was almost offended when she ended her diagnosis with a reminder that I was not gay. I was in agreement that prior to my building a friendship with Mickey I had not thought or seen myself in the life; however, I felt as if Mickey was stating that I wasn't serious when speaking on my true feelings. "How do you know?" I asked, and Mickey simply said that she knew. I was almost relieved when hearing Mickey even though I felt inside that she found my feelings to be a joke. I wasn't sure why I was beginning to feel the way I did but I thought that since Mickey had just as many years in the homo lifestyle as I had in the heterosexual lifestyle, she would know better than I.

Summer had finally come, and I found myself excited to end all the phone babble for some real time with Mickey. I looked forward to seeing her again and hanging out. I had realized that I spent all my time either working or on the phone with Mickey. I had not gone out in months, and the only other outing I did have was going back to Bristol to visit Nanny. Nanny wasn't aware of my new friend, and I had no desire to speak about her to Nanny. Honestly, I was hoping Nanny's prophesying gift didn't chime in at any minute when I was around her or on the phone with her, exposing my feelings I was having inside for another woman. Always very aware of Nanny's gift and very scared of it, I made sure not to even ignite the possibility by saying Mickey's name, speaking on the topic of homosexuality, or even being around her too long to sense anything. Nanny's gift was strong and nothing to play with!

Mickey and I had made plans for me to spend the weekend out her way, so I took the weekend off, packed a small bag, and took that forty-five-minute drive west once again. You would have thought that we hadn't seen each other in years when I parked at her mom's house. I waived at her best friend who had made it there before me to welcome her home and then gave Mickey the biggest hug anyone could. We all decided to go to the bar and celebrate, though I wasn't sure what for. When we got to the bar, I found out that Mickey was moving closer to home. She decided to take a basketball opportunity closer to Clarion. I was so excited to hear it because I had decided to go back to live with Nanny who was in need of my help with my uncle, which would have made our distance much more convenient with her move back to Pennsylvania. It was definitely cause for a celebration, and we did just that with all the alcohol and MJ that we could tolerate without passing out.

Though we were completely intoxicated, we made our way safely back to the house laughing and giggling about anything and everything. We made it to the room without waking anyone, and Mickey turned on Power 99 while we had a few wine coolers to end the night. We started talking about how much fun it was going to be with her so close. We could hang out more, and I could finally see these indescribable skills that everyone seemed to go crazy about. As we went on and on fighting our sleep with wine coolers and laughter, we found ourselves closer than we had ever been physically and emotionally. Our hands touched as we sat on the bed, and we both sprung our hands away as if we had offended one another. I couldn't hear the music any longer as our laughter turned into a silence that once occurred in our past over the phone, but this time there was no phone to hang up and nowhere to run. We both had to confront each other as our bodies reacted to feelings that had been balled up for months without expression. Our thoughts and feelings for one another became so obvious as we gave into a bodily reaction to those feelings and we engaged accordingly. As the night went on, I began to understand why I wasn't able call Mickey back when I told her I missed her. I understood why I had so much need to hear her voice every day. I realized why I was so excited to hear that she was returning to Pennsylvania for good. For the first time, I was indulging in a desire that was building up inside of me since the first day that I met Mickey. In that night I had opened a door that was intended never to be unlocked, and by the time I realized what I was getting myself into, I was at a climax of mixed emotions. As I exhaled, my face was filled with tears of shame, my mind was filed with confusion, my heart was empty, and the only thing I could do was cry in the arms of what I felt was my future.

She had no idea what was wrong with me as the tears ran down my face and drenched her shirt. I lied to Mickey claiming that I was just being emotional and blamed some of it on the drugs and alcohol, but it was much deeper. As Mickey was trying to figure out why I was so upset, I was trying to figure out how I had gotten to this place. Was this what I wanted and the example I wanted to be for others? "It must be my heart talking," I thought. There was no other reason for me to keep going on. I had opened my heart to a love that I was unfamiliar with and so scared. I didn't know if I made the wrong decision, but everything inside of me told me that I was not heading down the right path. I felt my eyes puffing up from all the crying, and I felt so drained. Mickey stopped asking questions and just held me saying it was okay. I didn't want to look at her because I was afraid that I would give away the disappointment I had in myself, so I just laid there in her room and closed my eyes.

By morning all that I had experienced from the night before hadn't left me as I hoped it was going to. I wouldn't open my eyes, thinking that if I could only think really hard, I would open my eyes and be back in my room. I knew that wasn't going to happen, but it didn't hurt for wishful thinking. Instead, my mind played the night before over and over again, and I couldn't help but to get out of there as quickly as possible without alarming anyone. I had to think. I had to find myself, and I had to get away from Mickey. After the night I knew something was wrong. Everything was there from the feelings, the thoughts, and the physical attraction; however, Mickey was a girl. A girl! What was I going to do with that? What was I thinking and what have I started? "Was this the outcome of my disconnect with God?" I thought. I don't remember our conversation that morning. I just said anything appeasing not to make it seem as if I thought she had done something wrong. This was her lifestyle, not mine. I entered it head first, playing with fire, and now the burning was not tolerable. As soon as she hugged me outside of my car, I couldn't jump in quick enough and drive away to filter my thoughts. I drove to Clarion in dead silence, and forty-five minutes later, the only thing I could come up with was that I wasn't sure if I was interested in what we had started, what was happening to me, and what this experience could mean. All the answers that should have been no were yes all because all things in my life that should have been a yes were either jacked up or dead. What was so wrong with trying something new? What was so wrong with giving in, I thought, but I knew it was wrong. I knew that this was not what I was taught nor what was really in my heart; however, I had already committed an act that I couldn't get away from. I knew that I was going down a dark road, and I didn't care any longer. I wanted to be happy, and when I thought about it, recently I was finally feeling again what it meant to be happy. I was finally smiling more, feeling better, and not finding my pillows soaked from the tears I shed each night. I already knew that this was not going to be easy, but for the sake of all the hell I had been through already, there couldn't be any hell worse. At least that was what I thought!

If I had any doubt in my mind about going forward with a relationship with Mickey, she gave me one when we spoke on the phone again. She told me, once again, that she knew I was not meant for her world, and she was fine with us being friends. She explained that one day I was going to have a husband and children and forget about anything associated with her lifestyle. She explained her feelings for me and though right there I was being given the golden key to move on and away from what half my thoughts felt was a big mistake, I realized that the other half of me had found a feeling that I couldn't explain. I respected her honesty and feelings for me. I cared that she opened up to me, and though she developed feelings for me was willing to ignore those feelings for my wellbeing. I actually found it to be sweet and unlike what a man had done for me ever. I was blessed with young men in my life that did care about me but didn't treat me the way I expected and desired. Not even the last man in my life had enough love in his heart to fight for me, so why was I so caught up with the idea of being with a man? The ones I tried to date after Shay were selfish, most had nothing going for them, too old, too young, not serious, or just not for me.

I also could not ignore that my feelings had grown for Mickey. She was an ideal person for someone like me. She had dreams and ambition. She had been through hell and did not let that hold her back. She was a fighter and

cared enough about me to let me go. At that moment I realized that though she might have been willing to ignore
her feelings, I was not ready to ignore mine. I couldn't let
go of her friendship because if it wasn't for her friendship,
my depression would have continued. If it wasn't for the
time we had shared together so far, I would have been in
a completely different place in my life, and though I was
experiencing something that I had never given thought to,
I had to try. Anyway, how easy could it be to go back from
the act that Mickey and I committed? I felt like my fate had
already been determined, and I was at a point of no return.
There; my decision was final, and Mickey and I officially
became a couple.

CHAPTER 5

Living the Life

1 Corinthians 6:9 (NKJV)

"Do you not know that the unrighteous will not inherit the kingdom of God? Do not be deceived. Neither fornicators, nor idolaters, nor adulterers, nor homosexuals, nor sodomites."

Mickey and I had been together a few months, she was comfortable in school, and I was back at home with Nanny working and helping to take care of my uncle. The long-distance relationship was good for the both of us because we were both able to focus on our future. I had taken some college classes at the community college near us. Though I was actively working in a salon, I was interested in finding a different passion. I wasn't sure what it was. I just knew that I never possessed the competitive nature that one needed on the east side of Pennsylvania to hold one's own in cosmetology. Too much fighting over clients and price points that I simply had no drive in me to work for. I did hair because I loved doing hair, not because I was searching for riches in it. If I was looking to make better money, I would have stayed back West where I was making $3000 to braid hair and taking clients with a much higher financial wealth and a loyalty to their stylist.

I regretted moving back to Bristol, but the only thing that kept me moving was that it wasn't for me. I was there to help my Nanny. She could have taken every desire from my spirit, and I still would not have found a fault in it because she had always been there for me. So, I found myself back on the phone on a regular basis with my significant other. Just like with Shay! Another one of these relationships; however, the biggest differences were that Mickey wasn't across the ocean, and she wasn't a man. Though my feelings hadn't changed for Mickey, they also had not grown any deeper. The family had met Mickey, and some knew what was going on while others had their assumptions. It was easier to hide our relationship because she was so far away. I wasn't telling the parents, Nanny, or anyone else who I knew was going to try to put me in my right place. I figured if I got myself into all this, I really needed to get myself out and not hinder everyone else with worry because of my decisions. I wasn't ready for the exposure. I had enough just from everyone's assumptions. Plus, Mickey never pushed me to tell a thing. She agreed in public that we were only friends and never put me in a situation that forced my hand to speak out what I felt to be our secret. Instead Mickey and I showed our affection behind closed doors when we had the opportunity to see each other and over the phone.

What I found to be odd was that no one seemed to care about my friend selection. I guess with all the time I had spent away from the family being raised in the military, they probably thought this was my norm. Even without the trumpets sounding and a full coming out of the closet, I expected there to be more attention on Mickey's appearance and much more questions about her in general. As noisy as the family seemed to be about everything, I received much less attention about my current situation. It was a relief all the same time. I couldn't imagine the response I would have; still I expected that I would need one. My Nanny would ask me about my old boyfriend from high school occasionally, and I would say that we were just friends, and though I tried to date, the ones I was dating was not the ones for me. I would tell Nanny not to worry about me, and she would quiet down for a while and then ask me again later.

Though I didn't have the backbone to tell my mother anything about my situation, she knew, and she had no problem telling me how she felt in her always tough approach, direct yet indirect. My ears were open, but I could not come to a good mind to tell her about my hurt. My explanations would turn into arguments that I was not able to mentally handle. Instead of attempting to open up, I found myself defending Mickey and her situation. I knew in my heart that I was not meant to be in this type of relationship, but I could not question Mickey's reasons. She had been through so much and with all she was forced to withstand, if she found happiness in women, who was I to judge. The more I did defend Mickey, the more I found myself drawn closer to her. I wanted to be there for her. I wanted to be the one that understood and not leave her in her time of need. I found myself even more willing to continue in the relationship because of the lack of pushback from being in one. I was always feeling as if I needed to justify to myself reasons for staying with Mickey. Occasionally she would ask me if I really wanted this. There were times that she would just look at me and tell me that I looked sad, that I would be happier without her and with a man as it should be. During those times I would find myself fighting her on the comments she would make, and it would shut her up for a while. Later the questions would resurface, and Mickey and I would go back and forth with my confused response that I wanted to be part of our relationship.

As confused as I seemed to be there were still some rewarding things about my relationship with Mickey. I felt as if we understood each other much more being two of a kind. No explanation for that time of the month, mood swings, and when we were both on an emotional high it was wonderful. Staring at each other without any words yet with pure satisfaction was something that I had not experienced with a man. And those times that I really needed to be held and comforted were simply given without question, tears, or an argument as to why there was no attention to my feelings. The pros of being with a woman were greater than I could have ever expected, and they were addictive. I found myself lost in comparing apples to oranges and instead of truly finding a deeper reason as to my true attraction, staying surface level was more comforting.

Since this lifestyle was never a topic of discussion in my childhood, I didn't give it much thought, but since I was willingly a part of it, I began to wonder if my fate was the reason why Shay had left me. Maybe I had confused myself thinking the norm was for my life. Maybe men were simply to be a friend and not a lover. Maybe babies were meant to be for everyone else, and I was to be the babysitter. Adoption was also an option, though I never had the desire to adopt in my past. The thought of Mickey's and my relationship going further made my mind circle around so many possibilities of life I had not thought about before. Why did I never give myself the thought to open up to love in all areas? Mickey was a kind-hearted person, treated me well, didn't push me in any direction I wanted, and to make matters worse, she always tried to push me back into the world I once knew. She actually knew my heart better than I did. I could justify my actions with any sob story I wanted, given any excuse of Mickey's background to allow me the comfort for my decision, and I could make myself feel bad for turning the other cheek and going back to what I once knew, but the truth was that I longed for something that she didn't give me. The love I had for Mickey was the type of love that a person had for friend who was always there. I wanted to be there for her in her time of need, but not share a bed with her. I wanted to laugh, cry, and push through hard times by her side, but not as her lover.

I woke up one day and had to see her. I had to tell her what was truly in my heart. I had to confess the truth to her before I grew to hate her and myself. I picked up the phone and called Mickey to tell her that I had to come and see her. Basketball hadn't started yet, so she was available, and though I had a four-hour drive to her, with one call, she prepared for my coming. I told her that I might be there for the day or the night but that never mattered to Mickey. I drove down Interstate 80 one last time to what could have been the best or worse mistake of my life. If this was meant to happen, I would find myself happy later in life with a husband and children, but if I was making a terrible mistake, I could end up alone or in a much worse relationship later.

I was always one to think of all scenarios so I wouldn't be surprised of the outcome. It had worked for me up to that point, but as I drove, I wasn't sure. I started feeling my heart sink and my mind becoming more confused. I stopped midway for gas and thought about turning back to give it all another thought. I wasn't going to her because she cheated on me or me on her, and there was no excuse other than my experiment was over. I couldn't call it anything else. I knew Mickey wasn't going to accuse me of such a thing. I knew that after I spoke to her she was going to understand, but that was how I felt. It was as if I was playing with someone's heart and though I was also a part of the time wasted, I was taking time from another. I continued my drive and began to feel the tears rolling down my face as I thought about the times we had spent together. About the first time we met, about how much of an odd ball we both felt with our family and friends. Our laughs and crying. For a little over a year, Mickey's ears became my golden gateway to release myself. I didn't want to lose that but couldn't see how after this conversation we were ever going to go back to be friends. Still I got off at the Clarion exit and passed the Super Walmart on my right to head down toward the college. I drove up to the dorms and sat in the car wiping my tears, fixing my make-up, and trying to find the right words before I called her to say that I was downstairs. I knew that the time of procrastinating was over, and I had to find the boldness to love her enough to tell the truth. I picked up the phone and called her so that she could let me into the dorms.

When Mickey came to the door, she had that big smile on her face that she always had. She gave me a hug and a kiss and took my bag as we went to her room. I packed because I wasn't sure if I was going to stay. We caught up a little since it had been a while that we saw each other face to face. She knew something was wrong but couldn't get it out of me. I wasn't ready to reveal it. I wasn't ready to break her heart. I wasn't ready to possibly make the wrong decision. Instead, I lied and told her that just needed to see her to spend some time. We got some food and walked around a little talking about the updates of our families. She asked about Nanny, as always. She loved Nanny so much, but who didn't?

After all the preliminaries were out of the way, we tried to figure out something to do, but the bar, walking around Walmart, and just strolling around the campus wasn't very interesting at the time. Instead we decided to take up another past time, roll up and have minor session with our good old friend MJ. Almost instantly the anxiety I was experiencing had left me, and I was able to relax in Mickey's arms while we watched a movie. Not making the matters better, I had kicked off the shoes, got comfortable and made a night out of munching, smoking, and watching movies. Not at all what I had planned to do, and since I had gotten so intoxicated, my hormone levels were through the roof, and I found myself in another circumstance that I had not intended to be in. I found myself in the same situation that I was in the first night we spent together. Confused with tears running down my face I continued on as if it was simply one of those highly emotional, life-changing experiences that would change my heart and mind forever, but I knew better. I felt sick to my stomach for the person I had turned out to be. I felt worse because my feelings had not really changed for Mickey, and the entire reason for making the trip to Clarion was fogged by an overnight fling. I got up the next morning rushing out as if it was that morning I woke up in her room back in her hometown. I can't remember the reason I gave but I knew I had to get out and go home. We kissed, hugged, Mickey took my bags to the car, and made me promise to call when I got back to Philly.

The drive back was horrible. I couldn't have explained how I got home that day. High as a kite and eyes as watery as an ocean, I felt nothing but pity for myself. I was hopeless without a clue to how I was getting out. I had no outlet! I couldn't call anyone and vent about my desire not to be with my lesbian lover any longer. I'm sure some was waiting for me to say that I made a mistake and that I was an emotional ruin. I'm sure others wouldn't judge me at all, but I didn't trust what would be said behind my back, so I took the four-hour ride back down Interstate 80 alone, ignoring Mickey's calls and heartbroken. I hated myself, and I was beginning to remind myself why I was in the situation I was in to begin with. All the time had passed, and I found myself still blaming Shay and God.

This could have all been avoided, and now I had no idea what I was going to do. I'm sure if I went home and called Mickey to explain, she would think I was a nut case, but I really didn't find myself to be any better of a person than a nut case. Mickey deserved the truth, and I had to be the bad person in this situation. I couldn't make something up to make myself look better. By the time I drove into the car lot at Nanny's, I knew what I had to do. I was going to call Mickey and be truthful about the entire situation, but instead I called her and told her that I had made it in and didn't really hear the phone while I was listening to music. I said how great the time was we had spent together, and I would try to get out there if I could. All lies! I just needed to find the time to get up the nerve to tell Mickey that our night together was the last.

A few days after our last night together, I couldn't continue to hide any longer. Mickey basically knew and explained to me that she understood. I assured her that there wasn't anyone else and that I simply didn't see myself with a woman for the rest of my life and didn't want to continue in a lie. Mickey made me promise to find a good man because that was what I deserved. I couldn't believe the encouragement from Mickey. She drove with her heart, and I drove with my curiosity, and still Mickey loved me enough to let me go. Without a fight, argument, or leaving me with a guilty conscience, Mickey told me that she loved me, and I meant it when I told her the same. This exchange of love I believed was finally the correct way between her and I. Just friends, and it felt so good!

Mickey's and my phone talks were much lighter, yet still very comforting. Neither of us had significant others but were dating and the understanding we had of our friendship didn't limit us to having such discussions. It was as if we had been friends the entire time, we had known each other, and what I thought could have been an awkward friendship seemed to work out. I had gotten a job at the airport in the new TSA government positions opening up in the airports across the country and was so happy not to play the fake competitive hair dresser any longer. I had stopped driving to Dubois to do hair, so Interstate 80 had become a part of my past along with many other things. The classes I was taking at community were a little difficult because I had not had those types of subjects since high school. Hair school was much easier, and though I could have thought that time to be a waste of time and money, I appreciated the time I spent on my own. I was still very immature to relationships and love but getting much better at handling myself as an adult.

Nanny and I had a great thing going on. We didn't seem to bother each other, and we were able to spend some time together that we both felt we missed out on not being close to one another as I grew up. With the TSA job, I felt much more grown up. I had a full-time job with benefits all before the age of twenty-three. I was making decent money and trying very hard to pay bills on time.

Philly was a different world for me. The people were much different than the royal folks I had known all my life. Even military brats have a different lifestyle than a civilian. I was very ignorant to the city life. I tried going out to clubs and hanging out in the city, but that wasn't working for me. It was all so different. I even tried to hang out with family members going to college, but our maturity levels were on opposite ends of the spectrum. It felt different already having a career compared to my peers who still had one to two years before they were looking for their first "real job." I guess being with Mickey for that time slowed up my adulthood and allowed me to be careless in decision-making, thinking I had all the time in the world to grow up, but since I had started the TSA job, I felt like I was there. I was either spending time with people that were career-driven like me or hadn't made it yet, and juggling the two drove me crazy. I had no interest in drinking and driving, smoking blunts while walking down a Philly street as if I was daring a cop to stop me, or partying at some over-filled, childlike club shaking my behind as if I was trying to get a feel on the dance floor. Germany was years behind. Without spending so much time with Mickey in that world, I realized that I was more grown up than I thought. So, I took my job seriously as well as dating. I figured if I was going to stay in TSA until college was over, I should really take dating seriously as well because after all I had been through, the one thing I did know was that I didn't want to be alone.

Dating turned into an undesirable job like back in DuBois and Clarion. I couldn't stand the men I was meeting. They were either only interested in having sex, spending my money because they didn't have a job to make any of their own money, or couldn't get out of the rapper mentality. I didn't understand what it was that EVERYONE wanted to be a rapper or get rich quick! Considering rap was not at all my choice of music, and I felt like I was getting so old, though I was only in my early twenties, I became very frustrated with Philly, Bristol and basically every part of Pennsylvania. I'm sure it wasn't just the state I was born in that was the problem. I was also definitely sure that my choice in exploring the forbidden lifestyle was a good clue as to the punishment that was before me. My male selection in my past was nothing like this. I had better judgement of men over a phone conversation in my past, and now it seemed to be taking me a few weeks just to figure out my hand-picked selections were full of it.

After a few months of trying I found myself giving up and just focusing on me, and it seemed to be going well. I was focused on school. I was pushing myself at work looking into opportunities for promotions or even to transfer in my position to another location. I was hanging out with the family a little more when I wasn't working. I had even made a new friend at the job.

Kela worked in the baggage section of the terminal

on the lower level. I worked in the same section but on the second level for passenger screening. I had seen her around and not that often, but there was something about the way she carried herself that made her seem familiar though I had never met her before. Once we noticed each other more often, realizing that we had the same shift, it was difficult to keep ourselves from staring. I didn't know why I found such interest and was overly fearful of the thought the lesbian in me had not left, so I took every precaution to ignore her as much as possible. After a few weeks of just staring and looking away, I finally smiled on the parking lot transportation bus and said hi. The time it took to get from the airport to the parking lot, I found out that Kela lived right down the street, had just been through a divorce, and spent a few years in the military. I was most interested that she had just gotten out of a divorce because it meant that she was straight, which was all I was interested in being around. After hearing a little about her background, I finally understood what was so familiar. Military soldiers or brats all have a very distinguished character that seems very familiar. I told her a little about myself as well and left out any connection to the lifestyle for both of our benefits. We exchanged numbers and made arrangements to share a lunch break at work when possible. I finally had someone that I could relate to, I thought, but I was clearly mistaken.

It didn't take too many lunches at work to find out that Kela kept her closet days secret from me as well. I thought her soldier-like demeanor was what I saw in her; however, I found myself attracted to her, and it just made me crazy. Kela was much further in the single life than I was. She had her own place, her own life, furniture, credit score, money, and was taking care of her uncle in her own apartment. Being around Kela made me feel more like one of those immature young adults I had put down so quickly. I loved Kela's determination to be somebody, yet I felt for her because she had a story of her own. She was in love deeply, and her husband really played with her mind, heart, and money, leaving her with nothing much but a broken heart and a strength around everyone other than him. I would listen to her on the phone when he would call and just get sick to my stomach how she would turn into jelly when he said hello. Divorced yes, but you could hear and see the control that he still had over Kela. I couldn't stand it, and every time I would see his number come across the phone or hear her talking to him, I had to leave.

I always had a problem with people taking advantage of another person even though I felt like I did that to Mickey. This was different. It was as if he knew exactly what he was doing, and my anger for him and men like him made me sick. Kela thought I was jealous and made fun of me about it, but that was not the case. I had no intention of being anything other than friends with Kela, and though I was growing an attraction for her, I did my best to fight it. It wasn't jealousy. It was disgust that such a strong person could allow such a man who had already done so much negative in her life still put her in such a vulnerable situation. I was happy just to know their distance ensured that he had no real access to her so he couldn't be of any real harm. Even if it was a little jealousy, I couldn't let Kela know that. I was sure that the lifestyle I left behind was behind me for a reason.

During my off time, I found myself over Kela's house more often. She lived closer to the job, and I felt free to think and feel my way than compared to what I felt others wanted me to while centered around the spectating family. Kela had her uncle there, but he was working on getting himself together and not concerned much with her life. Kela also had a brother, and God only knows that I wish I had met her earlier in life. If I would have met Kela a few years prior, maybe we could have been sisters instead of friends. Her brother was so sexy, but taken! Some chick her brother had known for a while and went to college with. They both graduated, got married, and decided to have a baby immediately. Beautiful family!

I was around Kela and her family more often and less around my own. I had actually stopped dating after Kela and I had become friends, and I didn't want to admit to myself that I longed for her when we weren't around each other. My family was moving on with their own lives, in their own relationships, and I was standing still in between a crossroad that I had not chosen for myself. I couldn't believe that I took it as a surprise when Kela and I hugged each other one day and went way left field into a kiss and a situation that I had not planned for. I could not figure out what was wrong with me. As hard as I tried, I couldn't seem to keep away from these feelings I was having. What I thought I had made my way out of, I found myself back into the same situation. The life was actually becoming consuming and taking over all of me. Instead of me finding my way out, it was like I had taken one of those U-turns that one takes when they are unsure they are going the correct way. Instead of following the inner instinct of keeping straight, you find yourself turning around and going far enough back to start over again without starting from the very beginning. I felt as if I knew what I was getting into but couldn't seem to keep my feelings under control, which was the main reason why I gave it thought to see if Kela and I were meant to be friends or something more.

Kela was much different from Mickey. Kela had a bolder spirit, and there was no need for her to hide anything. She was accepted by friends or family if with a woman or man. Her ex-husband was the only person I noticed she made sure to show her vulnerable side with. With him I was a friend, but it seemed with everyone else she wanted a title that I had not even made up my mind to give to her. With me, Kela wanted to be more recognized as my close friend. She wanted to be known by everyone, which I never cared either way and though she never admitted being my girlfriend, I found myself arguing with her about coming out as if she needed a debut party.

We found ourselves in a relationship after a few months of being friends, but I wasn't happy. I just didn't know how to say no to her or I. I wasn't sure how to tell a person who had been a great friend to me that we needed to stay friends. I also didn't know how to believe that this life was not meant for me. It seemed as if the pieces were all adding up. Men weren't what they used to be to me. When I did date, I couldn't find a single thing that would keep my interest longer than a minute, and I had yet to find a future in the eyes of any man since Shay.

I was so sick of comparing my relationships with Shay that I felt desperate to just be with anyone who could make me at least a little happy and hopeful. During those depressing times I wished that I had not ended it with Mickey. At least she really cared about my wellbeing. Kela seemed to care but her motives seemed to be off. Kela and I went much further in a relationship than Mickey and me.

We had moved into an apartment together close to my side of the family, we both left TSA and got different jobs, and she was even going to the same college as I was. People say to be careful what you wish for. I found my desire to be in a promising relationship, but I guess I wasn't specific to mention that my desire was to be with a man!

CHAPTER 6

Getting Out

John 8:34-36 (NKJV)

"Jesus answered them, 'Most assuredly, I say
to you, whoever commits sin is a slave of sin.
And a slave does not abide in the house forever,
but a son abides forever. Therefore if the Son
makes you free, you shall be free indeed."

Kela really wasn't that bad of a girlfriend. I was more ir-
ritated with myself to feel so stuck in a situation that I put
myself in but couldn't seem to get myself out once again. I
felt like a drug addict failing miserably to recover. I would
get into small arguments with Kela and find the way out,
just to be swept off my feet again by the soft words of
"I love you." Even when that didn't work, and I had the
upper hand, I still found myself to be filled up with mixed
thoughts about how much we had been there for one another and the need to give it another try or at least stay
friends.

Friendships never worked out because it always led
right back into another relationship. I couldn't pick up the

phone and make a call to end it as it was with Mickey. We were a part of each other's lives, so it wasn't as easy to just end things. There were arrangements that needed to be made if we were going to end it. We were living together, working the same job, and I was depending on her to help me even drive around because I no longer had a car. Our dependency was on one another through all our tough times, and honestly Kela had the upper hand with the car, the most money of the two of us, and even the freedom to be who she wanted without hiding in the closet. I wanted to be in the closet because I was sure the lesbian life was not for me; I just couldn't seem to get out.

Kela was also such huge help with my family. She played a big sister role to my brother when he was going to school, helped Nanny and I with my uncle, and never asked for anything in return. By the middle of our relationship I felt more obligated than attracted. I just wish I had thought of that obligation when I first made the decision that I had feelings for her. I came to realize that it wasn't a real attraction but a need for companionship that turned to friendship and then lust. It was hard to find the way to break up.

I didn't really see Kela as being happy herself. She was beginning to change her appearance. When I first met Kela, she was a girly girl like I was. I guess that was why I would have never thought she had a desire for women. She always had her hair done, and we even wore the same types of clothes sometimes. I always wanted to be cute. Well into our relationship, I found her wearing baggier jeans, bigger shirts, and her micro braids turned into long cornrows that turned into just her own hair cornrowed. She already had that military look about her that no soldier ever seems to lose, and it was not at all attractive to me. I know Mickey had that same hard look, but I thought to myself all the time, "If I wanted to be with a man I would be dating one." The truth of the matter was that I did want to be with a man. I began to resent Kela for what she was not instead of pushing myself to own up to my confusion and get out and be who I really wanted to be. I felt so embarrassed to be such a coward!

Kela and I continued our relationship; however, I finally moved out after the lease was over. I was happy, and with less time together, I was able to think about my needs and wants more without the excuses and pressure I put on myself. Back to square one trying to decide what was best for me, but I began being distracted by other things. When I got sick, I started to really take my future seriously because I was being told by doctors that the future I did have wasn't too bright. I guess for most people, life in general would be enough, but not for me. There were no such thing as life to me without children and taking pills for the rest of my life just to be well was too much.

Doctors diagnosed me with Graves Disease, and the world alone was devastating to me. It wasn't as bad as it sounded; however, for my age it still was bad. I was told that what I had was a rare case for a twenty-four-year-old girl. I was told that most people diagnosed at my age were told they had hypo- or hyperthyroidism, but for some reason my levels were through the roof. Graves was my first diagnosis and the highest one of its kind. I just happened to be about twenty years younger than the normal women diagnosed with it. I was also told that I had a very low chance of having children because of my hormone levels, and if I did conceive it would be a challenge to get through the first trimester without having a miscarriage.

Hearing all this for the first time made me so scared and upset. I was even more upset that after a few months of the medications, I didn't seem to have any improvement on my test results. The medications I was taking were too many daily to see no improvement, and though my own Nanny had hyper-, she was diagnosed much later after children, so the effect was different. I was so distracted by the doctor's appointments and dealing with the symptoms, I forgot that I was fighting through an identity crisis. I began to think more about God and all that I had experienced over the few years since Shay had passed. I missed out on so many opportunities, experiences, and happiness because I was so caught up in a situation and lifestyle that I had not asked for and never desired. I then thought that the Graves Disease was my punishment for my ignoring all that I knew to be the right way. Why would God want to give a person like me a regular life when I messed up what he had already given me? Why would God give me children when I was trying to build a relationship with a person that couldn't conceive a child with me in the first place? Why make my life be easy when I spent so much time running from the only one who could make it all better? What makes it worse is that I knew God and spent almost five years of my life acting like I didn't know Him at all. Why didn't I speak up? Why didn't I ask for help?

I knew that I was getting exactly what I deserved, and there was nothing I could do about it. In the deepness of my heart, I longed to feel the desire of a man, but I knew that I didn't deserve a good man and was sure that God felt the same way. The Graves Disease placed me in a place of depression that was different from what I had experienced with Shay. I no longer felt like the victim and a lost soul who was forced to be the way I was. Instead, I was the reason for my depression. I could have lived a life without sickness if I had followed the way that I was taught. I could have been engaged or even married if I would have understood that everyone had their time to be with the Lord, and Shay's time was just meant to be before mine. I would have never questioned my identity if I was never so bold to dive into an unknown situation. My mind filled up with shame and guilt, and through it all, I still would look up and see Kela there.

Kela motivated me, helped me and even came in to see me when I took my radiation pill, even when the doctors said to stay away from people. It was nice that she was there, but I didn't want her there any longer. I didn't want anyone in my life that was like poison. I wasn't blaming Kela at all for what I was going through. I knew it wasn't her fault, and I knew that all I was undergoing was me. Still I didn't want to confuse myself any longer. I wanted to be alone and deal with the fact that I was meant to be alone. I wanted to live the best I knew how and deal with whatever God had for me. I didn't know how to say sorry. I didn't know how to ask for forgiveness. I didn't know how to begin a prayer to God who knew all things, knew I would make all these mistakes, and knew I would be fighting with myself through it all at the end. I just decided that since God made the decision to put me in a place that not even a decent man would want me, that I could at the very least show how sorry I was by trying to just deal with my life alone. No women, no men, no one! I was just going to work and mind my own business, and around all those I knew, I would try to be the role model I should have been from the beginning and be happy and strong.

With all the doctor's visits, spending more time with Nanny, and working in my new job to open a new hotel in the town next to me, I didn't realize that my lifestyle was changing. I wasn't seeing Kela as often, and she was living her life. I couldn't fall into the trap of confusion again. For some reason I knew within myself that whatever was meant to happen in my life, the LGBT life was not the life for me. Making any moves towards it was like playing with fire and taking ten steps backwards. I was still very fearful that I would be living a lonely life; however, I came to the conclusion that whatever God had for me I was going to accept because literally my life was in his hands. Results weren't changing much for my thyroid and my doctors continued to encourage me to keep up with my pills, which were at some very high dosages, because they wanted me to avoid the possibility of getting worse.

I replaced the depression of comparing my life to what it could be if Shay was living to researching the disease that I was diagnosed with. I was not at all convinced that this was the end. That at such a young age I was going to be taking medication for the rest of my life. I found that the addiction spirit I thought I possessed because I couldn't seem to get away from women, was purely selective. There was much of my life that was changing and did not define how an addict would react. I wasn't drinking as often, smoking as often other than cigarettes, and I was becoming okay with spending some real Leah time and not looking to fill holes in my broken heart. I wasn't missing Shay any less, but I was beginning to appreciate who he was in my life. I also began to recognize that it could have been me. God spared my life when Shay's was taken. It could have easily been the other way around. Shay was ready to go home; however, I was coming to realize that I was not. If it were the two of us in that car that day, where would I have gone? Was my mind in the right place to have been called home by the Lord? At that time, I didn't even have a good mind to trust God and in His own will for me and Shay. I blamed God as if I was the one who wrote out my destiny. As if I was the one who placed myself on this earth and had a right to make any decision I wanted and still expected to go to Heaven to be with the Lord.

I was too blind to see why Shay was placed in my life. I was too much of a child to realize I had a lot of growing up to do, and Shay was only one of the first steps to that development. As I took the time to really think about Shay and God without the hurt and hate that I once had, I was able to see what Shay brought to my life. Shay opened up my heart to recognize a good man when I saw one. A man that didn't think of himself in every situation but was willing to sacrifice his own happiness to see another's. Shay could have encouraged me in my young adulthood to stay in Germany with him, to begin a life with him, and put my plans on a back burner. Instead Shay taught me that when you love someone, and you have faith in God, you stop trying to plan a perfect life but trust the process.

I learned that there is no real time in love. From the time I met Shay until the time he died was a total of nine months. The number nine spiritually represents divine completeness! Divine completeness! God completed Shay's time on this earth, but it took nine months from beginning to end to understand that some of my plans, expectations, and judgments on life needed a new thought process. What he was meant to do here was done, and I couldn't accept that what our relationship was meant to do was also complete. I had to accept that Shay was not my soul mate because if he was, we would have married before his death. God would have made a way for that to happen if it was in the will of God regardless of Shay's or my decisions. Instead, God allowed us to be together for on those nine months for a reason, and as I thought of all the good times I had with Shay, I also thought about all the hell I put myself through simply because he went away. The transformation in my feelings for Shay and God became the highlight of my days. Inside myself I was so sad because I knew I had messed up so bad, but I couldn't help but to be thankful. I was beginning to realize that I was making excuses to continue my wrongdoing. I could have stayed in my mess and never owned up to my faults, but what good would that have done?

I found myself thanking God in secret for so many things from my past. My deliverance was beginning before I noticed it, and I found myself happier than I had been in a while even being alone. I wasn't convinced that God would give me a husband due to the sinful acts I had committed. I didn't deserve a husband, but if I could be happy not settling for women just for pleasure, I would be okay. I wasn't exactly sure if I was going to heaven or hell, so I didn't want to hinder some man's walk with God because of what I had done in my past. I remember in my past thinking that if I was going to go to hell anyway, I should be happy here on earth and just deal with the lifestyle that I knew was not of God. It didn't make me happy to be with women, but I was comforted not to be alone. I couldn't say that life wasn't fair any longer because I knew I was hiding behind the excuse to justify my actions. I made the decision not to lie to myself any longer, but the truth hurt. I had to just face my consequences, and God knew I was terrified to die thinking my eternal life was hell, but I tried not to let that hinder my walk—in life and with God. I gave so much to the devil, and regardless of where I was going to go, I had a made-up mind to at least try to do my best with my relationship with God and live the life that was designed for me.

It felt good to be around the family more often, and though I still was not very fond of Bristol, I made the best of it. One night while hanging out with the cousins, I met a guy name Nate. He was very quiet and seemed to be a loner, still he was so cute and reminded me so much of Shay. It wasn't in his looks or his voice but just in the way he carried himself. Nate had a lot of family he was surrounded by all the time; however, he seemed to be set in his own ways. He didn't talk much and didn't seem to have much interest in anyone, but his sister wanted so much to see him settle down. I heard he had not one child but four! Back in the day, four children would have been enough to send me on my way and not even go back to my cousin's house for a long while, but that didn't seem to bother me any longer. I always wanted to have my own children, but Shay taught me that if you truly love someone, you love everything about them.

I didn't know Shay's baby girl in person, but I knew that she was a part of him. I didn't question if I could love her, I just instantly loved her when I saw the picture of her. In that thought, I got the lesson the Holy Spirit had designed just for me back then to prepare me for my experience with Nate. I figured that if I were to be with a man again, I could easily love four children if back then at such a young age I loved one child. Nate was older than I, which didn't seem to shake me because Shay and I were eight years apart. Nate apparently had some bad experience with his children's mother which was oddly the same situation that Shay had with his daughter's mother. Over a short period of time what I learned about Nate seemed to be more like deja vu from my past and honestly was a little scary. What was happening? I started to over-think, and after exchanging numbers, talking on the phone, playing hard to get and having our first date I was in awe about this Nate. It wasn't an immediate love connection, but it was a possibility that I didn't think would happen in my life again. Nate made me smile, he made me laugh, he was just as screwed up in the heart and mind as I was, but there was a fight in him as well that had him still pushing. I liked him and began to desire more time with him.

We did the traditional dating, meeting of the family and children, and as I was half responsible for what seemed to be the fast-paced relationship, I couldn't help but find discomfort in my dishonesty. He never asked me, and I wasn't even sure if he was aware, but I struggled with if Nate had the right to know what type of relationships that I was in prior to meeting him. Did it matter so early in our relationship who I once was? Would it matter if I never did anything wrong in our relationship if I never told him? I had so many questions and concerns and didn't know what to do about them. After some serious thought and fear that he would find out from someone else and be mad that I didn't say a word to him, I decided to explain to Nate as much as he needed to know about my life. I told him about my life in the lesbian world and though I never really had the desire to be with women, I made the choice just the same. I was surprised when Nate told me that he heard it already but really didn't see that in me. I couldn't help but to be reminded of when Mickey would tell me that the life wasn't for me and that one day, I would meet a man and be happy. Nate's main interest was that I wasn't still interested in women, which I made it clear that I was not. And so, I was back in a real relationship with a man, and not just any man, a decent one!

It didn't take long for Nate and me to find our way into an apartment together. By our six-month anniversary, we had found a place between Nanny and his mother's house. Perfect for us to grow but stay close enough to the family. Not too much longer, the children moved in with us, and we had a ready-made family. The first year was one of the hardest years I could have ever experienced. The move-in was premature, but Nate and I both felt that we were ready to make a commitment to one another and wanted to show the children that we were serious about one another. We both had a lot of faith walking to do as a couple, but most importantly as individuals.

At first it felt as if everything was going so fast. Though we had moved in together, before the end of the year we were talking about marriage. Nate had come into the relationship with trust issues, and I had come in with a lack of faith. Still we depended on each other to be encouraged and inspired. Many days what we had brought to the table from our dark past got caught up in the whirlwind of our relationship, but we had a fight in the two of us that would not die. It is fearful when things seem to be too perfect to be true. We didn't have the best life, but together it was more than I could have hoped for. I wondered many times when looking at our relationship, how did I get to the place I had gotten to? I even searched for the problems to justify my disbelief of deserving of what I was experiencing. While questioning my current situation, doubt began to enter my thoughts. I wanted to believe so bad that this was the life I was meant to lead, and that God was giving me another chance, but doubt invaded that belief. It was going too fast, and I thought that maybe I was going to be to Nate and the kids what Shay was in my life. Just a chapter in their book!

Nate and I began to talk about how fast our relationship was evolving once we exchanged the "I love you" with one another. We continued to talk about marriage and how our life would play out. Often, we would sit down in our almost empty apartment talking about our future and find out even more paired facts about one another. Nate and I both shared a desire to help young people. We really didn't understand how that was going to happen, but we spoke about counseling opportunities, being part of a boys' and girls' club, encouraging young people that went though the wilderness as we did to help them come out. We also spoke about our love and how it all seemed to work out through the mess we had gotten ourselves into. We found out very quickly that even our faith and the upbringing of our faith was much alike. Nate was more church-raised and my foundation was home-taught, but our belief in God was strong.

As strong as our families were in their faith, we didn't fail to admit to the mess we created when old enough to make up our own rules and laws. Though we spoke deeply about our regrets, we always came back to what God had done in our lives to keep us from so much more heartache and even death that we could have experienced. Knowing that I wasn't in life alone in my faith increased my love for Nate and the kids but also scared me even the more. I wanted to be prepared if God decided to take my life. I didn't believe that a man as good as Nate deserved to take a chance of marrying me, and I was sure that God would take me before messing Nate's life up. I never told Nate because I didn't want him to think I was crazy. Instead I kept those type of thoughts to myself and attended church every so often with Nate and the kids. I continued to pray that the Lord would help me find peace in my past and acceptance of the life I was experiencing.

It was a Sunday morning that Nate and I were getting ready for church that I felt something a little differently. While we were in church, the Holy Spirit was so high that one could easily believe that anything that day could happen. That day no demon would have tried any trickery, and you knew every prayer was being answered. Nate and I sat in church side by side together and enjoyed the word as our apostle preached. Periodically, I would look to my right at Nate and smile as I thanked God for what he had done for me in my life, for brining Nate into my life and showing me His love. I wasn't prepared to leave the earth and still at that moment scared of where I was going if the good Lord took me away, but I couldn't help but to appreciate that I would leave the earth knowing how good God was to me and how I woke up every morning just to the one example of a God-fearing man by my side. I wasn't engaged, there were no promises that we would make it that far, but still everything felt right.

We were still in sin, shacking up, but the direction I was going in compared to where I last was, was beyond improvement. I recognized that. I recognized God. Through the sermon I kept looking at him and in the different aisle where our children were as visions filled my head of what it would be like if we were to marry. I knew that it would be no easy task, but I wanted it so bad. I knew then that it would work out if given the opportunity. Nate and I fit together! As my mind filled with so much joy of God's gifts to me, I came to notice that I wasn't paying attention to the word that was being preached. Another mistake that I had to ask forgiveness for, but I was watching the word manifest right before my eyes, and it consumed me and placed me on a spiritual high that day.

Romans 10:9-10 (NKJV)

"...that if you confess with your mouth the Lord Jesus and believe in your heart that God has raised Him from the dead, you will be saved. For with the heart one believes unto righteousness, and with the mouth confession is made unto salvation."

Suddenly, it was time to stand as a congregation, close our eyes and pray as the apostle asked if anyone wanted to come up for prayer. This was our chance to give ourselves to the Lord or resubmit ourselves to the Lord. I knew in my heart that I had given myself to the Lord in the hospital bed almost two years prior before I even knew who Nate was, but there was this feeling inside myself that wanted so badly to move. I wanted to thank God openly and freely to the world and recognize in public what he had done in my life and that He is Lord. I knew no one understood, but I didn't care what people thought or knew; I just wanted to thank Him. Right before I was about to nudge

Nate to ask him to step aside so I could make my way to the front, I felt Nate's hand grab ahold of mine. I looked down at his hand just to confirm that what I knew to the touch was confirmed with my eyes and then I looked up at him. Without words, we smiled at one another and he led me to the front of the church hand and hand.

As we took the few steps we needed to reach the front of the church, I started to think about what it took to get to that very moment. Within myself I was stepping into a destiny that I couldn't see, but in that very moment I knew that every step afterwards it would be with Nate. I was beginning to understand that my wilderness was not meant to hinder me to confusion but prepare me for my future. I knew I was holding hands with my husband though I had not gotten my ring nor was the question asked of me yet. I knew his children also belonged to me, and even if there was ever any doubt about me being their mother from anyone else or even from them, that thought would never enter my heart. I knew I was stepping into God's will walking side by side with the gift that only God could have handed to me. We made it to the front of the church, and when I closed my eyes and said the sinners prayer, I knew that I had a lot of growing to do, but this growth was meant to be with a man that I would share that growth with as long as God had me on this earth. With tears rolling down my face, God removed the doubt in my heart for a chance to make it to heaven. He filled me with hope and faith. I was no longer was afraid of the outcome of my fate because I was then sure that God had me in his hands! My soul was finally free! I could breathe, exhale, and thank God!

It was almost a roller coaster ride following that wonderful day. Apostle made no promises of there being a great party, or our world transforming into a utopia for the rest of our lives just because we were recommitted to the Lord; however, the only promise that one could know is that God was with us all the way. As for me, my faith was growing stronger every day, and the only person I could thank for it was God. I began to see healing that I could never imagine. Windows and doors were opening before my eyes, and also some had closed, but it was all God's will. It wasn't too long after that Nate and I got engaged and married with our children in our wedding. It wasn't too long following the wedding that I received another gift from God as he opened my womb and blessed me with a child. Not too long after that we were blessed to become deacons. Even now while writing this book, we are nine years married and still going strong. We still have our challenges and face some tough times; however, we know exactly where our help comes from.

CHAPTER 7

Redemption

Ezekiel 36: 25-27 (NKJV)

"Then I will sprinkle clean water on you, and
you shall be clean; I will cleanse you from all
your filthiness and from all your idols. I will
give you a new heart and put a new spirit within you; I will take the heart of stone out of your
flesh and give you a heart of flesh. I will put My
Spirit within you and cause you to walk in My
status, and you will keep My judgments and do
them."

I would not have understood this scripture back then. I was
a victim to the entrapment of my own mind. I was a victim
to my own thoughts. I was a victim to my hardened heart.
I was a victim to my own silence! I didn't cry out to the
good Lord to save me from all I had endured, to take away
my pain, to lead me in the right direct, or to turn from my
sick ways. I was silent and in hate. My silence became a
statement because I knew if I would have just spoke up and
asked God to forgive me for all I had done, all the thoughts

I kept within me, all the actions I had taken, and all the decisions I had made, I knew that He would forgive me. Deep down I knew God would forgive me, but I was too ashamed to expose myself to Him.

My ears weren't open to the Lord, but I was listening to the enemy filling my head with lies that I could never be forgiven. The enemy said God would never hear my cry. He said my life would never be the same. He told me that if I tried to be with a man, I could even bring damnation to his life. The enemy told me that I should just stay in the lifestyle that I was in because hell was the only place I was going. The enemy! Faith had left me back in that dorm in hair school, and I wasn't wise enough to open my ears to the Lord. I wasn't wise enough to see the warnings that were in front of me. I wasn't wise enough to remember my first love. I wasn't wise enough to call for help. I wasn't wise enough to ask for prayer or search in the word for salvation. Back then, I wasn't wise enough!

Throughout my wilderness, I was a victim to silence because that was what the enemy wanted for me. I didn't realize that the only one silent in all this was me! God was pulling on me when I didn't go crazy in that dorm room back when Shay passed away. I couldn't see that the Holy Spirit was blocking my actions from my thoughts of suicide. The Lord was giving me verbal warnings even with the girls that I chose to have a lesbian relationship with as they told me that I wasn't gay. I now understand that I made myself a victim to the enemy by making the decision to be silent with God. It only took me to open my mouth and ask for forgiveness. It only took me to recognize what I already knew about the salvation of Jesus Christ. It only took the minimal of me for the greatness of God to act in my life. In all that silence, I lost myself, and I lost my God. With a simple YES, God gave it all back!

We get so caught up in the way of the world that we don't know how to silence our surroundings to hear the Lord's voice. Instead we become silent to God and a slave to the enemy with no one to fight for us. Instead of taking the word for truth and finding our salvation in Jesus, we allow the enemy to fill us up with curses, sickness, pollution, idols, lifestyles, and bad decisions that were never meant for us to accept or experience. When we get stuck in these situations, the enemy fills our minds with ignorant thoughts that we can't make our way out. As a people, our belief grows greater in damnation than salvation! It's time to fight for the right we have as the children of God. Expose ourselves and our sins and find the good news in Jesus Christ. With repentance and accepting Jesus as our Lord and Savior, at that very moment, our sins are washed away, our hearts are made new, and we don't have to be silent any longer.

Luke 19:10 (NKJV)

"for the Son of Man has come to seek and to save that which was lost."

This testimony is for the lost because that is where I was! Living a lifestyle outside of the word of God will only lead to pain, suffering, and separation from the Savior. One of the hardest things I could accept for myself was to really believe that I could be forgiven. I have always felt that no sin is greater than another; however, when you are in an act that you can't see light in front of, it is very difficult to see yourself out and moving on to something better. If you would have asked me in my early twenties what was I doing, I would not have been able to say that I was going down a dark path without any hope to return. I didn't see what God had in store for me and didn't believe that He wanted anything to do with me any longer. I didn't understand that salvation was meant for a person like me. The lost! I was so lost, caught up in a tangle of thoughts. Fighting within a lifestyle that was never meant for me and losing my natural mind.

However, I took an experience of a trial in Shay's situation and turned what should have been my growth into damnation. I didn't stop to look in the word and understand that my patience was being put to the test. I didn't cry out to someone for help. Instead I was filled up with prideful thoughts that I had to be strong for the world as I was dying inside. How foolish was I to think my thoughts alone were facts? Even when I opened the Bible, all I saw was the separation of myself from God instead of the salvation that is offered to all sinners through Christ. It took the Lord to pull me out of my state of mind and place me into a mind of holiness to see that forgiveness was a gift promised to the ones who believe. Sometimes I think about how hard God worked just for my soul. He could have given me up a long time ago. All the people of this world, and He took time out to see about me even when I didn't want anything to do with Him! That is a love that is immeasurable, and there is no thankfulness great enough to show the Lord my gratitude. So when I was asked by my cousin why did I choose faith, God, and fully committing to Him now after over twenty years on this earth, I was very genuine to express to her that I gave way too much time wasted as a victim of the enemy. It is now and forevermore time to give all that I can to the Lord, only!

My prayer is that one will find their way to understand that God loves us all. God loves you! There is nothing too hard for God, nothing he can't fix, and there is nothing that he can't take away. Our hearts are hardened by our own choices. It could be a dramatic change in our life plans like mine, an upbringing that was not favorable or fair like Mickey, life gone wrong like Kela, or another reason that pushed your spirit to the edge. Whatever the reason, there is hope in your future because you are still living and breathing the breath of life. There is light in front of any darkness, and God is that light that can and will get you through the darkness if you choose not to be silent and ask. Don't be confirmed to this world! We are only here for a very short time, and in that time, there are so many great things we could be doing that is all open for us to read about in the word of God. We have to get a true understanding of our purpose in this world and not confuse it with what we want to do or be. We must get back to the word and find the purpose the Lord gave to us when he placed us here on this earth, when He planted our seed within our mother's womb and sprinkled it with His water by way of our fathers so we can sprout and become what He intended us to be.

We must be careful to say things such as, "God made me this way." That was my excuse for everything to justify my actions with the thought of God knowing what I was going to do before I did it. Though there is nothing in disguise when it comes to the Lord., our choices are our own free will to walk in the way of righteousness or to walk in the flesh. There is a difference, however. The Lord honors our choices. When I made my decision to step into identity confusion, I made that choice wholeheartedly and became a slave to it. I must confess that it was my choice. I must acknowledge that though the Lord knows all, I didn't ask Him was it right or was it righteous. I didn't go to the word to get confirmation for every footstep I took, so I can't blame the Lord when I order my own steps. I just acted in my own ways and thoughts, becoming completely consumed with it. At one time it was like being a drug addict. When you hear stories of how you want to come out and just can't, it can be very difficult to do things on your own without the strength of the Lord. It's time to choose a side!

Psalm 46:1 (NKJV)

"God is our refuge and strength, A very present help in trouble."

He is our refuge!

He is the condition in which we are safe and sheltered, from pursuit, danger, or trouble.

He is that feeling you get deep down inside when all hell is going on around us, and we feel as if we are comforted without explanation. When we need home, but we are not tangibly able to reach it or get to it fast enough, still we find ourselves housed in the middle of four walls with a foundation and a roof that confines us from everything outside of ourselves. We see rain of fire around us; however, we notice that we are not drenched with small droplets of scorches from the fire. We notice chaos but aren't affected by it! Even when we are approached by another searching for the same shelter, we find ourselves able to open our door and expose others to this home that has been keeping us. The attacks, the dangers, and the trouble that move toward us are not victorious because the Lord has provided us the place of refuge!

He is our strength!

The quality or state of being physically strong.

There is a strength in God like no other. We see it in those times of challenges and doubt. When everything around us is showing that we will be defeated, yet there is a lion within us that won't allow us to back down. When we have to face a fear that we thought would kill us. When we have to fight pain to make it for our families. When we are told that we will never be anything in our lives but push to be the opposite. When doctors tell us that we won't live long, but we find determination to live out the rest of our lives as if each day is all the time in the world. When we lose something or someone so dear that we know there is no way anything could fill the losts; however, we find that loss to be a blessing in disguise. The Lord is the strength that keeps us physically able to keep on keeping on!

He is present!

In a particular place; Existing or occurring now.

He is here! As we read, as we breathe, as we sleep, as we live our lives. With every decision we have ever made, with every test we have gotten through, with every sin we have committed and been forgiven for, the Lord is with us! He was there when I lost Shay, when I wanted to hate someone or something so bad. He was there when I lost myself. The Lord was there when I was attempting to drink pain away and when I was filling missing gaps with terrible decisions that conflicted my mind. He was with me as I cried and was lonely. He was watching even when I thought he was not. God was there through it all, through each and every moment. He is with us all right now!

I could never repay the Lord for what He has done for me, my life, and most importantly my soul. I can only recognize Him and His goodness. I thank God for all that I have been through so far in my life. Even for what I am ashamed of because with His help I have made it through that time of shame. I thank God for His blessing over my life and not finding it robbery of His time to see about me. I thank God for the testimony that He has given to me to share with someone so that they as well know that our God is good and that His mercy is endures forever. Mercy is what the Lord gifted to me. When I didn't deserve it. When eternal punishment was what I should have received, instead I received mercy! What do you do for the Lord that has done that in one's life? There is nothing I can do other than to be thankful and remember what He has done for me. Nothing I can do but try to honor His love for me with doing and being my best every day. Remembering where I could have been when my flesh begins to act up, and it's time to set it straight. Nothing I can do but thank the Lord for it all.

I pray that this testimony touches the heart of someone that might have felt lost at one point of their lives. Might have found themselves somewhere that they didn't plan to be and fighting to get out. Know the fight is over with Jesus. Be free indeed and allow the good Lord to work a newness in you. Find your testimony through all you have been through by finding all God has done for you through the storm and how He led you out. If you still feel like you are in the storm, don't be a victim of silence as I was for so long. Speak up, ask for help. Pray for help. You will find that as soon as you begin to speak what you are truly looking for in your life, the Lord will reveal it to you. Believe that you have the right to want better. Allow your steps to be ordered by the Lord. Try Him! Seek Him! Silence can be so damaging when you are stuck in a situation that you can't find a way out. When our thoughts are distorted, it's almost impossible to find proper reasoning because we are in a lost state of mind. With a simple yes, a faith booster, and an open ear, you will find out how great God truly is. Kill the Silence!

May God continually bless your situation, your life, your family, and your home. Amen!

CPSIA information can be obtained
at www.ICGtesting.com
Printed in the USA
LVHW040719010920
664669LV00028B/1400